ANTIDOTE

ANTIDOTE

BREAKING CHAINS, BUILDING EMPIRES, FINDING REAL LOVE.

SUNNY MASTERPEACE

PALMETTO
PUBLISHING
Charleston, SC
www.PalmettoPublishing.com

Copyright © 2025 by Sunny Masterpeace

All rights reserved

No portion of this book may be reproduced, stored in a retrieval system, or transmitted in any form by any means–electronic, mechanical, photocopy, recording, or other–except for brief quotations in printed reviews, without prior permission of the author.

Paperback ISBN: 9798318803987
eBook ISBN: 9798318803994

PREFACE

**This ain't your regular self-help book.
It's a street sermon.
A love letter laced with war cries.
A survival manual for the broken, the betrayed, the real ones who stayed too long in places they should've burned to the ground.**

It's not sweet.
It's not soft.
It don't whisper healing — it demands it.

Some chapters gon' preach.
Some gon' punch.
Some gon' feel like a letter from the future version of you saying:
"Get up. I got you."

You might cry.
You might rage.
You might close this book and come back different.

And that's the point.

This ain't a feel-good book.
It's a feel-everything book.

This is **The Antidote**.

Read it like your life depends on it.
'Cause if you've been losing yourself in love that don't love you back?
It just might.

I didn't write this book to sound smart.
I ain't here to drop college words or play philosopher.
I didn't write it to be poetic for the sake of beauty, or philosophical just to sound deep.
And I damn sure didn't write it to blend in with the crowd or kiss up to the self-help industry.

I wrote this because **too many real ones—solid souls with golden hearts—are out here getting stomped on, thrown away, and forgotten like they never mattered**.
People who give with both hands, love with both lungs, and still get treated like background noise in someone else's story.

And I know that pain personally—'cause I was one of them.

I've been there.
I've sat in that silence.
I've laid in the dark wondering what the hell was wrong with me.

I've felt betrayal hit like a sucker punch to the chest that left me gasping for air with nobody around to see me fall.

I've stared at mirror like it owed me closure.
Waited on messages that never came.
Swallowed pride just to keep love alive—
And begged The Creator in whispers.

I never spoke out loud and say "please take the pain before I turned cold for good."

But sometimes?

Going cold ain't the curse—it's the cure.
It's not the death of who you are—it's the rebirth of who you were always meant to be.
I didn't walk out of that fire the same.

I came out **Stronger,**
Wiser,
Louder,
And more dangerous—but not to destroy others...

To **protect myself.**
To **rebuild** what I let others tear down.
To **reclaim** what I gave away for cheap love and validation that never deserved me.

This ain't about revenge.
This ain't about clapping back or proving anybody wrong.
This is about healing—in the rawest, and realest way possible.

The kind of healing that don't come wrapped in a cute caption, or hidden behind filters and fake peace.
This ain't a healing spa. It's a soul detox.
This ain't therapy talk. It's concrete truth.

This book right here?

It's **not polished**.
It ain't sweet.
It won't beg for approval, and it's not afraid to offend.

This is a **mirror**—for the broken.
A **blueprint**—for the bruised.
A loud, **unapologetic war cry** for every soul that stayed too long in places they should've **ditched, burn down and never look back!**

This book is for the ones who **loved too hard**,
Stayed too soft,
Gave too much,
And got played like they were nothing but a pit stop in somebody else's journey.

It's for the ones who **lost themselves** while trying to fix someone who had no intention of being whole.

It's for the **Kings** who forgot they were Kings—
And the **Queens** who gave up their throne for a few temporary compliments and some toxic attention.

It's for the ones who've ever sat in a room full of people and still felt like a damn ghost.
For the ones who gave light to everybody else and now can't even see their own reflection.

You've been sleeping on yourself.
They had you doubting your own shine, begging for crumbs, forgetting you were the **whole damn feast.**

Well now?

Now it's time to **wake the hell up.**
To **wise up.**
To **rise up.**

And to walk out that door—head high, heart armored, crown straight, and **soul on fire.**

I didn't write this book to save you.
I ain't your hero.

I wrote it to **remind you—**

To remind you that, You were the damn savior all along.

Contents:

- Preface v
- Prologue xiii
- Acknowledgments xvii

- **Section 1: Detaching from Unhealthy Relationships 27**
  - Rule #1: Stop Waiting 27
  - Rule #2: Know Your Damn Value 47
  - Rule #3: Walk Away Smooth (W.A.S). 69
  - Loved Wrong, Left Right 84
  - Played Low, Rose Solo 95

- **Section 2: The Queen's Code 113**
  - Rule #1: Respect the Real 122
  - Rule #2: Be Modest 132
  - Rule #3: Master the Code of Compassion 142
  - Rule #4: Lock it with Confidence and Love 156
  - Laced in Love, Locked in Loyalty 172

- **Section 3: The Kingdom of Boundaries 185**
  - Rule #1: Never Reward Disrespect 192
  - Rule #2: Guard Your Peace 201
  - Rule #3: Don't Share Too Much 210
  - Rule #4: Don't React with Emotions 221
  - Rule #5: Be Willing to Walk Away 229

- o The Unwritten Chapter: After the Walk 234
- o Love With Lines & Structure, Not Lies & Secrets........236
- o The Crown that Waited, then Walked 243
- o The Queen that Refused the Cage 253
- o When You Can't Fully Walk Away: Reality Check 266

- **LOVE AIN'T A GAME — IT'S A KINGDOM.... 268**
- *(Part I) The 7 Tests to See If They Built for Tru Love* 268
  - Test #1: Will They Ride or Bail When It Rain?..........................269
  - Test #2: Are They a Mirror or a Mask? 269
  - Test #3: Ten Toes Down or Playing Both Sides? 270
  - Test #4: Can the Silence Hold or Does It Break? 270
  - Test #5: Same Path or Split Directions? 270
  - Test #6: Can They Lead Without Ego and Follow Without Shame? ... 271
  - Test #7: Is This Legacy or Just Lust? 271

- **Part II: 7 Tests to See Who Really Rocking With You — Tru Homie Edition** 273
  - Test #1: Is Their Loyalty Loud When You Ain't in the Room?...273
  - Test #2: Can You Bleed Around 'Em and Still Feel Safe?...........273
  - Test #3: Do They Clap for You When It Ain't Their Turn? 274
  - Test #4: Are They Solid or Situational? 274
  - Test #5: Will They Call You Out Without Tearing You Down?. 274
  - Test #6: Can They Hold Water or Do They Spill Tea? 275
  - Test #7: Are They There When There's Nothing to Gain? 275

- **Final Word: The Throne Is Yours (The Legacy Begins)** 277
- **Letter to My Old Self** 285

PROLOGUE

There comes a moment…

After the games.
After the lies.
After the pain's been rinsed and repeated so many times, it don't even sting anymore—it numbs.

That moment when you stop chasing closure, stop replaying conversations, stop crying in silence.

And something in you just… **snaps**.

Not in rage.
Not in revenge.
But in **truth**.

It don't come with fireworks.
It don't come with tears.
It comes in the quiet—when you're standing alone, staring in the mirror, and suddenly seeing everything that's always been there…
The strength. The Royalty. The warrior.

The one who kept showing up while being ghosted.
The one who gave endlessly, loved fearlessly, and still got treated like an object.
The one who watered dead gardens hoping they'd bloom, not realizing some hearts only grows weeds, and not the good kind.

That moment right there? That's where this book begins.

Because *The Antidote* ain't no fairytale.
This ain't no bubble bath of clichés or fake positivity wrapped in pretty affirmations.

This is war medicine.
This is a **street sermon against the snakes venom,** born from silence and soaked in sacred rage.
It's a **survival manual** for the ones who had to grow a backbone where their heart used to be.
For the ones who learned how to **smile with a broken spirit**, and **stand tall with a stabbed back**.

This ain't healing dressed in white robes.
It's healing dressed in scars and steel.
It's truth that don't whisper—it kicks doors in.

Every chapter in this book was carved out of heartbreak.
Each word sharpened by betrayal.
Every lesson baptized in disappointment and dried off with fire.

But it's still written in **love**—
Not that soft, scripted love you see in movies.
But that *get-up-off-the-floor, wipe-your-tears, fix-your-crown, keep-it-moving* kind of love.
The love that don't coddle you—it **challenges you to evolve.**

Because you were never meant to stay broken.
You were meant to **break through**.

So if you've ever been:

- **Ghosted,**
- **Gaslighted,**
- **Lied to,**
- Or treated like a damn backup plan by someone who had no idea how divine your energy was—

This book is for **you.**

If you ever showed up with full heart and clean hands—
And got hit with games, silence, excuses, and recycled lies—
This book is for **you.**

If you ever sat in your room, overthinking what you did wrong,
Blaming yourself for being too much, or not enough,
If you're sick of holding on, sick of apologizing for your standards,
Sick of being **chosen last** when you should've been the
first and only—

This right here?
This is your **line in the sand.**

This book ain't just paper and ink.
It's a switch.

And once you flip it?
There's no going back to begging, shrinking, or doubting.

So go ahead—
Take this Antidote.
Sip it slow.
don't look back.

Because the old version of you?
The one that tolerated disrespect?
The one that bent over backwards for people who wouldn't even meet you halfway?

That version?

Already buried.

And the real you?

Rising. Crown Straight. Flame lit. Soul, Untouchable.

ACKNOWLEDGMENTS

For the Roots That Held Me Down and the Storms That Made Me Grow

Before you turn another page, I need to pause and give **real love, real thanks, and real flowers** to the people who helped make this possible. Because this book—*The Antidote*—didn't just come from me. It came **through** me, built on the shoulders of those who held me up, pushed me forward, and stood tall when I couldn't.

This story, this journey, this fire—it wouldn't exist without the people who stood by me and the ones who walked away. Both shaped the man I am. Both left their fingerprints on these pages.

To my mom and pop—

You are my roots.
The two pillars who never folded, even when I did.
You stood firm when the winds blew wild.
When I was lost in the noise, you were my silence.
When the world turned its back, you opened your arms.
Your love never had endings.
Your support was never based on my success.
You loved me through the storms, and you believed in me before I believed in myself.
I owe you everything.

To my Two Older Sisters, and my Big Brother—

Even though the miles and years have stretched between us, know this: you were, and always will be, the bedrock beneath my feet. In the darkest chapters, when I was fighting battles no one saw, the knowledge of your existence, of the blood runs deep, was a silent strength that held me down.

You taught me resilience before I even knew the word, and in the chaos of my own journey, your unwavering spirit, though distant was a constant beacon. This Antidote to the poisons, carries the echoes of everything we've went through as a family. It's a testament to the power of family, a silent vow that no matter the distant or the time. The love remains. Thank you for holding space for me, for rooting for me from afar, and for simply being who you are. We may not see each other everyday, but our bond is a forever kind of unbreakable. This one's for us.

To Natalie—

We had fought many battles together and sometime against each other, but that doesn't erase the truth—
you gave me my two greatest blessings, Ben and Tonio.
And through life's twists and turns, you brought Isaiah into this world, and somehow, my heart made room for him too.
Three boys. Three legacies. Three reasons I'll never stop fighting.
No matter where the years take us, I'll always honor the fact
that you were the one who brought them here—
the ones who will carry my blood, and my hope for a better tomorrow.
That's not small. That's not something I could ever overlook.

You gave me a gift no success, no money, no dream could top—
the title of Father.
We've had storms. We've had silence. We've had distance.
But between all that, there's an unshakable truth:
those boys are the best parts of me,
and you are part of the reason they're here to change this world.
For that, I give you respect.
For that, I give you love.
For that, I give you thanks.
And for that, your name will always be written
in the roots of my story.

**To my Three boys—
Ben. Tonio, and Zay**

You are my reason.
My heart. My breath. My fight.
You are the rhythm in every chapter, the fire in every line.
I wrote this book so y'all never have to question your worth.
So you never have to shrink to fit in, never have to bleed for love
that won't heal you.

You can walk with your heads high, knowing your value isn't
based on who accepts you—it's based on who you are.
You are my greatest creation, and everything I do is to leave
behind something stronger than struggle.
This is your legacy.

To Jacksen—

You might not share my blood, but you've always had my heart.
You're like a son to me, and your presence in my life has been a
quiet blessing that speaks volumes.
Thank you for your kindness, your loyalty, and your love.
Your spirit reminded me that family isn't always about DNA—it's
about who shows up and holds you down.
You've given me strength in moments when I didn't even realize
I needed it.
I'm proud to have you in my life, and I'll always have your back.

To Patricia. L—

You didn't have to. But you did.
You showed up when it mattered most.
You stood in the gap and made sure that I see my boys when life
tried to rip everything apart.
Your strength didn't shout—it showed up in your actions.
You gave with no expectations.
And for that, I will always have love and respect for you.
Thank you for bringing me what I love most when I couldn't
go anywhere.

To Christina. R and Monica. R—

You both stepped into the storm when I had nothing left to offer.
You didn't turn away from the dark—you walked straight through

it beside me.
You didn't just listen, you lifted. You didn't just talk,
you **showed up**.

You helped take care of my kids when I couldn't—
and **that** right there?
That's not just love. That's legacy. That's family.
You became safety nets when the world felt like it was
falling apart.
You made sure my boys felt covered, seen, and protected.
You became a light when I was ready to stay in the shadows.
You reminded me that even Warriors need rest, even Kings need
grace, and even the strongest can break…
but they **don't have to stay broken**.

You helped me find my way back, not just for me—but
for my sons.
You both helped carry the weight, and I'll never forget that.

To Kevin Washington, my mentor—

You didn't sugarcoat. You sharpened.
You taught me that clarity is power and discipline is freedom.
You didn't just hand out wisdom—you demanded evolution.
You made me own my identity, stand on my name, and move
with intention.
You taught me how to lead with presence, not ego.
And in a world full of noise, you helped me tune into my
inner voice.

THE ANTIDOTE

To Tommy Bletcher, the One-Eight OG—

You didn't just teach me how to be a Boss—you taught me how to be **independent.**
How to stop waiting, stop begging, and start building my own lane.
You reminded me that I don't owe anyone my silence, my struggle, or my delay.
That I can be both humble and unstoppable.
You helped me stand tall when everything else around me was shaking.
You gave me tools when all I had were open hands.

To my brothers behind bars—

To **S.K, Hakeem, TJ, DJ, Quick, Big-E, Bono, Yohannes, Red, Chris, Smoke** and the many more whose names might never get printed but whose strength never goes unnoticed—
I see you. I salute you. I ride for you.

This world tried to break you.
The system tried to silence you, forget you, **erase** you.
But you're still here. Still breathing. Still fighting. Still **rising**.
You are warriors forged in fire—proof that even behind steel doors and concrete walls, greatness still grows.

This book is for you.
It's for your pain, your silence, your strength.
For every struggles you endured, every tear held back, every

dream deferred but never denied.
You are not forgotten—you are **foundations**.
Your resilience shaped this message. Your voices echo in every line.

You are not your sentence.
You are not your charges.
You are **Kings in the making**—and when the gates open, the world better be ready. Word up!

And to every exes who broke my heart—

Thank you.
Yeah, you read that right.

Because without your betrayal, I would've never discovered my boundaries.
Without your silence, I would've never learned to speak life into myself.
Without your games, I wouldn't have recognized what peace truly feels like.
And without your absence, I wouldn't have reclaimed my throne.

You didn't destroy me.
You revealed me.

You didn't end me.
You **elevated** me.

You made me question myself—and then I found answers no one could take away again.

So in a twisted way, this book is a gift wrapped in your rejection.
A crown forged in your disrespect.
A healing birthed through your chaos.

This book is for all of **them**.
And it's for all of **you**—
The readers who are tired of bleeding for people who never even brought a bandage.

It's for the ones who stayed loyal while being lied to.
For the ones who gave it all, only to be treated like they were never enough.
For the ones who questioned their worth because someone else couldn't see it.

No more.

This book is a thank you to every scar that became scripture.
To every loss that became a launchpad.
To every "no" that forced us to build our own "yes."
To every heartbreak that handed us back our power.

So now—turn the page.
But don't just read it—**feel it**.

Because this ain't just a book.

It's The Antidote.

And once you drink from it—
You **never go back** to being soft again.

SECTION 1

DETACHING FROM UNHEALTHY RELATIONSHIPS

This is about cutting ties with the poison.
Recognizing when love is just control in disguise.
We gon' teach you how to spot manipulation dressed as affection,
and how to walk away smooth—no drama, no warning,
just quiet power.
Because sometimes, the real flex ain't fighting back—it's never turning around.

We've all been there, caught in the spin cycle of BS, feeling like a hamster on a wheel going nowhere fast. You ever notice how some folks are like emotional vampires, sucking the life right outta ya? They leave you feeling drained, like you just ran a marathon in quicksand. That ain't life, that's a slow bleed. Recognizing that toxic tango is the first step to freedom. It's like finally seeing the cracks in the pavement you've been tripping over. Maybe it's that "friend" who only calls when they need a favor, or that family member who thrives on drama. Whatever the source, if it feels like a constant drain, a weight on your chest, a storm cloud hanging over your vibe, that's your gut screaming, "**Red flag!**"

Breaking free ain't easy; it's like untangling a knot that's been tightening for years. But peep this: your energy is your gold. You can't afford to keep investing it in dead-end situations or people who treat your spirit like a doormat. You gotta be a ruthless gardener, pruning anything that ain't helping you blossom. Think of those toxic ties like a leaky faucet, constantly dripping away your precious peace. You gonna keep putting a Band-Aid on it, or are you gonna shut off the main valve? If it ain't feeding your spirit, if it ain't adding fuel to your fire, then it's time to **cut the cord**. Snip that lifeline with conviction. Your soul ain't a charity; it deserves to be nourished, not depleted. It's time to reclaim your energy and build a life that actually fills your cup, not empties it. Remember, your peace is **non-negotiable**.

Rule #1: Stop Waiting

Waiting for a toxic person to change? It's like holding out your hands in the rain, begging for bread—when you've got the power to build your own bakery. Stop holding on to something or someone that's just wasting your time. You ain't an object. Your are a human being with real feelings. Get off the sidelines and bust a move, fam. Life's too short to wait for anyone to see your worth. Your value ain't a damn question mark; it's an **Exclamation point!** Period.

Rule #2: Know Your Damn Value

If you don't know your worth, then you're just a diamond in a pawn shop. Stop letting people haggle you for less than you're worth.

You're the prize, not the consolation prize. This rule is about realizing that your worth ain't something that's handed to you; it's something you claimed with **Confidence** 'cause you own it, you worked hard for it. You've gotta believe you're worth the best, or you'll get stuck settling for whatever is left on the table. You ain't nobody's damn option; you're the damn **choice**. Own it.

Rule #3: Walk Away Smooth (W.A.S.)

The word (**WAS**) turned the meaning of the sentence into past tense. Let that sink in for a sec! Some folks don't know how to leave a situation with class. They make a scene, cause a scene, and burn good bridges they can never cross again. But a real Royal? They burn necessary bridges and walk away smooth. No drama. No second-guessing. It's like this: you ain't gonna stick around a club that ain't vibing, and you sure as hell ain't gonna stay in a relationship that's draining you. Walking away isn't quitting; it's **choosing yourself**. You don't need to explain, beg, or chase after someone who don't appreciate your worth. You just dip out. You leave with your head high and your peace intact. If they didn't see your value, that's on them, not you.

SECTION 2

THE QUEEN'S CODE

For the women who forgot who the hell they are.
For the Queens who let crowns slip chasing clowns.
This ain't about being louder or tougher—it's about being *unshakable*.
It's about reclaiming your respect, demanding and reclaiming what's truly yours (power and peace) and **never folding to earn affection**.
You'll learn how to **walk in grace and slay in silence**, how to hold yourself so high that anything less than a Royalty feels like disrespect, and dismiss them with grace and class.

Check it. The game's been played one way for too long. The record's skipping, and we're dropping a whole new beat. It ain't just time for the Queens to step up; it's time for them to ignite. Forget the fairy tales, sis. This ain't about waiting for some glass slipper to fit. Being a Queen? That crown ain't handed out; it's forged in the fire of your hustle, polished with your resilience. You move like Royalty not 'cause you got a title, but 'cause your spirit commands it. Respect ain't given; it's taken through the sheer force of your integrity, the unwavering truth in your stride. Royalty ain't begged for with sweet talk and shady moves; it's earned by the unbreakable foundation you lay. See, your worth ain't a price tag you hope someone else sees. It's the diamond in your soul, cut with the precision of your self-awareness, gleaming with the brilliance of your self-belief. And best believe, you ain't just guarding it; you're the vault, the steel doors, the whole damn security system. And there's codes to it.

Rule #1: Respect the Real

Respect ain't just something you get; it's something you give first. Unless you wanna stand in the category of "most people" then you know you gotta be strong. A Queen doesn't have to force respect; she commands it with her presence. She walks into a room, and people feel the energy shift. When she carry herself with respect, she teach others how to treat her. She ain't gonna be loud or obnoxious; just standing firm in her self-worth. When she respect herself, others have no choice but to mirror that respect back to her. If they don't, they don't belong in her kingdom. Respect yourself!

Rule #2: Be Modest

Modesty ain't about shrinking yourself or downplaying your strength. It's about knowing when to let your greatness speak for itself. A Queen doesn't need to shout her worth; her presence does the talking. She's not out here flexing for the crowd; she knows her value and doesn't need external validation. Her power is quiet, but it's undeniable. The people who need to see it will see it, and the ones who don't? They're irrelevant.

Rule #3: Master the Code of Compassion

Compassion is the unbreakable bridge connecting every heart, from the block to the boardroom. A Tru Queen knows when to soften her edges, when to pour grace into a rough situation, and when to uplift her man, even when he's silent or the world is trying to tear him down. But her real power stretches further than just her King. She's got that vision to see the struggle in everyone she crosses paths with, honoring their grind and treating them with kindness, all without letting anyone ever mistake her empathy for weakness. This ain't about being a doormat; **it's the real flex**, a power stronger than any muscle, deeper than any wound. This is how you move.

Rule #4: Lock it with Confidence and Love

Confidence and love are the keys to a powerful relationship. A Queen locks her man in with trust, loyalty, and love, but she does it from a place of confidence. She ain't afraid to give her love, but she also knows her boundaries. She isn't out here desperate for affection; she's offering it with the confidence that she knows she's the best thing that's ever happened to him. Love ain't a game; it's a choice—and it's a choice she makes from a place of inner strength.

SECTION 3

THE KINGDOM OF BOUNDARIES

You are now on your journey of healing, so its important that you don't plant any poisonous trees in your kingdom again. For that you need Boundaries. And Boundaries are like the walls of your kingdom. Without them, people will walk all over you. A real Kings and Queens knows that boundaries are sacred. These boundaries define what you will and will not tolerate, and they protect your peace. You don't just survive; you thrive within your boundaries.

Once the wounds heal, you build.
But this time? With stone, not sand.
This section shows you how to build your kingdom and protect it—your heart, your peace, your purpose.
You'll learn how to draw lines that don't get crossed, how to enforce consequences without raising your voice, and how to **guard your soul like the crown jewel.**

Rule #1: Never Reward Disrespect

Respect is a two-way street. If someone disrespects you, and you let it slide, you're telling them it's okay to treat you like less than you are. Don't give people the green light to treat you like trash and then expect them to treat you like a Royalty. Disrespect ain't something you tolerate, it's something you shut down the second it shows up, but you don't need to be rude about it, you shut it down with class from a place of calm and confidence. If they ain't showing you that respect, they gotta bounce. Straight up. Ain't no sense in letting folks keep dishing out the disrespect and then acting like they can't live without you. Know your worth, fam. Let 'em step if they can't step right. You're a star, and you deserve to shine bright without no shade. Keep it moving with your head held high!

Rule #2: Guard Your Peace

Peace is a currency that's more valuable than any material possession. Once you lose your peace, everything else falls apart. Guard it like a treasure. People will try to steal it, situations will try to drain it, but you need to protect it with everything you got. Don't let anyone disturb your peace for the sake of their chaos. If they're bringing noise, you need to bring silence and let them figure it out. Your peace is your power. The one who is most likely to survive in the chaos is the one who don't panic, and flinch. In order to do that, you need that peace.

Rule #3: Don't Share Too Much

Your life isn't a damn open book for everyone to read. Some things need to stay locked in the vault. Don't give away your story to people who don't value it or who can't handle it. When you share too much, you give people access to parts of you they're not worthy of. Keep some things to yourself and only let the right people in. The more you keep for yourself, the more mysterious and powerful you become.

Rule #4: Don't React with Emotions

Reacting with emotions is like playing chess with a King and moving your pieces based on panic. You need to stay calm and make calculated moves. Even when you lose a powerful piece. Life will test your temper, and people will push your buttons—but if you can keep your cool, you'll always be ten steps ahead. If you don't like being the puppet on a string, then be the one pulling the damn strings. Don't let people control your reactions. The real power is in being unshaken, no matter what the world throws at you. You either operates as a prisoner or as a freeman, no matter the situation or circumstances, 'Cause believe it or not, it is simply a state of mind. The only way you're locked up is when your feelings control you and you'll be free when you can easily put a chain on them.

Rule #5: Be Willing to Walk Away

This is the ultimate flex. Be willing to walk away from anything that disrespects you, drains your energy, or pulls you away from your mission. When you walk away from a situation that no longer serves you, you take your power back. It's not about running away; it's about knowing your worth and not settling for less. If you've got to leave comfort, stability, or even love to protect your peace and your vision, then do it. A man or woman who's willing to walk away from anything that doesn't align with their purpose is the most dangerous force in the game.

Throughout this book, I ain't just dropping bars and motivational fluff. I'm handing you **weapons of wisdom**. Tools that slice through the fog of confusion. So, use it, but don't abuse it.

It's Time To Rise Up People!

"THE ANTIDOTE"

You gave your time, your heart, your flame,
   But all you got was silence and shame.

You waited on texts, they laughed with their friends,
   And left your devotion with no thought to mend.

You poured out your soul, hoping they'd see,
   The strength that was born from your loyalty.

But they made their choice, and it wasn't you—
   Now it's time, you choose yourself too.

Look in the mirror, speak it out loud:
   "I won't wear heartbreak like a shroud.

I choose my peace, I choose my worth,
   I won't beg love to prove my birth."

There are two types of souls who walk this land—
   One stays waiting, the other takes a stand.

They won't change, and that's their song,
   But staying in place is choosing wrong.

Their silence said what words would hide,
That you don't hold a place by their side.

You felt it deep, but ignored the song,
And wore a smile to mask the frown.

But pain ignored just grows in weight,
Until it breaks you, or you create.

Create a life where you are free,
From chasing ghosts of who won't see.

So let today be the day you part,
From anything that breaks your heart.

Detach with grace, walk firm, walk tall—
You never needed them to rise at all.

If you wanna be a slave, don't take this hope.
Otherwise fam, here's the Antidote!

Take a sip!

If you're feeling this poem deep in your chest, like it's speaking directly to your soul, then don't even think about putting this book down. If you're ready to take the lessons and apply them throughout your life, you're stepping into something powerful. It's not about being selfish, it's about learning to respect yourself enough to stop settling for less than you deserve.

Aight, the game is this Kings and Queens, so check it. You gave them everything. Your time. Your loyalty. Your heart. Your energy. You put your whole self out there, thinking they'd see the Royalty that you are. But what did you get in return? Silence. Disrespect, and pain. They played you like you were just an option, another name, like your value didn't even register. While you were waiting for a response, they're out there, laughing with their crew, living their life like your loyalty didn't even matter. And now you're stuck holding the bag, with nothing but the bitter taste of rejection. But here's the truth, fam. You don't need to stay stuck.

It's time to look at yourself in the mirror. Not with guilt, not with doubt, but with strength. You're not weak because **they didn't choose you**; you're strong for **choosing to stand tall, to choose yourself.** And the first step? Saying it out loud: "I CHOOSE POWER AND PEACE. I CHOOSE MYSELF."

It's like this. In this world, there's two types of souls. The Simps, the ones who beg for crumbs, the ones who stay on their knees, hoping their "master" flip the script and suddenly see their worth. And then there's the Bosses, The Royalties, The ones who take control of their own narrative. They don't chase; they elevate. They don't beg; they set standards. When the snakes shows you who they are, don't ignore it. Don't try to convince yourself they'll change. That's just your fear talking. Let them go. Walk away knowing that you don't need to tolerate disrespect (I mean real disrespect. Not no petty sh*t) or settle for anything less than what you deserve. This ain't about being cold-hearted or out here acting like you don't care. Nah. It's about building a life that reflects your worth. It's about self-respect. It's about knowing that your peace and your growth comes first. The real antidote? It's knowing that you have the strength to walk away, to let go of anything that don't align with your higher self. And when you do that, you'll see the world start to shift around you. The people who truly respect you, will rise to your level, and the ones who don't? They'll fade into the background.

SUNNY MASTERPEACE

Which one are you?

So, here's the real talk. take a sip of this Antidote, but don't rush it. Let these words sink in, because this is about a mindset shift. It's not just a temporary fix. This is about building lasting peace and finding real, deep satisfaction with who you are. You're not the type to beg for validation. You're not the type to stay in a situation where your worth ain't seen. You're the type who walks away with grace and strength, and because you understand that your life is too valuable to waste on anything that is toxic and doesn't contribute to your growth.

Now, as you sip on this homie, know this: there are real rules to this journey. You can follow them or not. It don't make any difference to me. I'm just a sincere advisor. But if you're choosing to build yourself, to level up, to take control of your peace and your life, then these rules are for you. And once you start living by them, you won't just change your life, you'll change everything around you. Tactics that let you stand tall when love tries to knock you down. You'll learn that **sometimes silence is the loudest scream**, and that **peace ain't a vibe—it's a war you win every day by choosing yourself**.

This book ain't about revenge. It's about **rebirth**.
It ain't about getting even. It's about **getting better**.
It ain't about proving sh*t to the ones who left.
It's about proving **everything** to the one who stayed—*you*.

So if you're tired of playing healer to people who only bring pain...
If you're done pretending you're "good" while crying in silence...
If you're ready to **bury the broken version of you and resurrect the savage King or Queen that's been trapped inside...**

Then, take this *Antidote*.
Drink deep.

And don't just read this—
Live it.

Are you ready to choose your power and peace? Ready to level up? Then read on, my Brothas and Sistas. Read On... Let's get it!

SECTION 1

DETACHING FROM UNHEALTHY RELATIONSHIPS

Rule #1: Stop Waiting.
(The Royal Command Over Time)

Straight up, cut that damn cord, fam. You out here holding your breath, waiting for a hurricane to turn into a gentle breeze? That ain't how the streets move, and that ain't how hearts work either. People, especially those who ain't built like us, they show their Tru colors from the jump, as soon as they get comfortable. **Believe that noise the first time you hear it, let that sh*t sink into the deepest parts of your brain.** 'Cause it ain't just a saying, it's a damn survival code, etched in the concrete, proven in every battle.

You keep rolling outta bed, thinking today the script flips? Today they gonna wake up and see the rare rock they're sleeping on? Nah, fam. Listen to the whispers. A real King, a Tru Queen, someone who sees your shine, ain't gonna leave you stranded in the desert like this, begging for a drop of their time, a crumb of their attention. Time and loyalty, that's gold in this twisted game of life and love. You throwing that valuable currency, your very life force, at somebody who ain't even looking at the damn price tag, who treats your worth like a discount bin item. I'm just here to remind you, in case all this heartache's got you forgetting the sovereign you are. And "Time"? That's the one thing they can't print more of, can't buy back. You pouring it out like cheap liquor for someone who ain't even sipping? Why waste it?

You think they're gonna pull a 180, turn that ice into fire one day? You're just bankrolling your own damn pain with fairy tales, calling it "effort" like you're getting a trophy for being stepped on. That's why your heart's cracking a little more every time they laugh in your face when you show your real side, ghost you when you need a shadow, then slide back in just enough to keep you hooked like a damn fish. It ain't 'cause they want your love, it's 'cause they want to own your spirit without putting in a single coin of investment. Keeping your loyalty locked down like a burner phone in their back pocket while they out chasing clowns who treat them the same dusty way they're treating you.

You ain't their lover, you their damn emotional emergency room. They run to your clinic when these other lames cut their ego wide open, 'cause your care is free and you're always open for business. Wake up, fam! You're worth more than being a damn pit stop on their road to nowhere. Start investing that time and love back into yourself. You're the real prize here. A real solid diamond rock. You don't wanna be out here stuck in the mud, just staring at the sky, hoping for some divine intervention, a damn lightning bolt to strike next to you so they suddenly get blinded by your shine. But peep this game, playa: **you're the one who dealt this hand. You're the one who showed them the rules.** You're let them know from the jump that you're a Plan B, the dusty spare in the trunk they can roll out when their main ride breaks down. I'm not saying this to make you feel bad. I'm letting you know so that you can wake up. sh*t… somebody gotta let you know. And if this little ass comments shook you then, you better hold on tight. 'Cause it's about to get really real.

Think about it, G. Every time they throw you a crumb of attention, a text, a late-night call, you right there, panting like a puppy. You showed them that their silence ain't gonna scare you off, it just gets your patience pumping, showing them you'll wait endlessly. They stab you in the back, and you put on a damn band-aid and give them a hug that they don't even respect. They puts in the bare minimum, and you throw them a damn parade of "I'm here for you, always." You basically gave them the cheat codes to your heart, homie.

The Truth About Change (And the Mirror)

And listen, Kings, and Queens. My Royalties, all that positive talk about people changing? Sounds good in theory, like a smooth rap. But in the real world, on these streets, folks only switching up when they hit rock bottom, when they look around and see that they done fumbled something real. They realize they lose a rare rock like you. That's when the light bulb finally flicks on, when reality hit and they realize they lost something they took for granted like air in their lungs. But, if you ain't got the strength to walk away, then they're never gonna see what they have taken for granted.

But let's keep it a buck, aight? You ain't really waiting for them to morph into some lovey dovey fairytale character. You're hiding from the damn mirror. You scared to face the fact that you gotta flip the script on yourself. It's easier to sit in the same old pain than to step into the unknown, to become the person who walks away. You dodging the cold truth that your loyalty been spilling. out on barren ground, your love been used like a worn-out mix-tape, and that deep hunger for connection? They weaponized that against you, turned your biggest strength into your kryptonite. You gotta break free from this damn cycle, homie. Silence that noise immediately. Stop looking outward for the change. The power's inside you. It's time to reclaim your worth, to see yourself as the prize you truly are. You ain't no spare tire, you the whole damn vehicle. Start driving your own life, playa. Don't just step into the unknown but Drive right into it. Feel?

Cutting the Cord: Surgical Precision

You've been out here thinking pain is the price tag for love? Like you gotta eat dirt to deserve a damn meal? That ain't hustle, that's just getting played, for real! Hurt without learning something, without leveling up? That's just straight-up foolish, keeping you stuck on the same damn block, going in circles, caught in a loop of your own making.

And every single time you try to lay out your heart, explain yourself to somebody who already wrote your story in their head, who already decided what your role is in their lives? You ain't just wasting your breath, you throwing your worth in the gutter. It ain't just about how they see you, it's about how you start seeing yourself. That's the real hit, homie. Not them walking away, but you refusing to lose yourself. Stepping the hell up, recognizing the King or Queen that you truly are.

Now, executing the real cutting off skills? That ain't about turning into some heartless robot, cold as ice. It starts when you stop chasing those damn fantasies in your head and look at the cold, hard truth staring you right in the mug. They ain't needing more time, they had all the damn seconds, minutes, hours, and damn days, and they let 'em slip through their fingers like sand. They ain't needing space to "figure things out." They took space like a damn thief in the night, taking so much space that N.A.S.A gon' be all up in there, claiming new territory. They did all that without a single thought for your feelings, your peace.

And clarity? Playa, their actions been speaking louder than any sweet nothings they could whisper. Every unanswered text? That's a damn message. Every blown-off plan? That's a billboard telling you where you stand. Every single time they made you feel like you ain't even in the damn picture? That's the truth tattooed on their forehead, clear as day, saying "you're just an entertainment." Remember that!

The Mirror and the Trap: Your Vision, Unclouded

You gotta stop trying to make deals with the reality that's written in stone, homie. It's right there in black and white, across every sign they've been throwing your way. You're an afterthought to them. You're on their radar when they want something from you. Time to wake up and see that for yourself. You deserve to be somebody's damn priority, not an option, not a convenience.

Despite all your grinding, and hustling, you're burdened by a heavy feeling you can't quite identify. You're staring in that mirror, seeing a fighter, a survivor, but something ain't right, is it? That fire in your belly feels chocked, that climb you're on feels like you're dragging anchors.

See that person beside you? The one you ride for, the one you bleed for? They're the trap homie. They're the haze that clouding your vision. You think they got your back? Nah, they're just leaning on it so hard that you can barely breathe. They whisper poison in your ear, telling you what you can't do, dimming your shine so theirs can look a little brighter. You're so loyal, so caught up in the drama, you can't even see the bars closing in on you for your lock up.

That mirror ain't lying. You got greatness in you. A storm waiting to break. But you gotta wipe that grime off your eyes. That ain't love, that ain't loyalty they're showing. That's a leech, sucking your strength, keeping you down in the dirt with them. Clear up that vision, soldier. See them for who they truly are. A weight holding you back from flying. You deserve to soar, to breathe that fresh air at the top. That ain't selfish, that's survival.

Here's the kicker my Royals. The trap door was never locked. They made you believe that you can't get out. They took away your motivation, your ambition and made you believe that you have no power to even reach for the door handle. They took away your hope by making you believe that they are the best you'll ever get. I'm here to give you back your Tru power. You deserve peace and don't worry about the happiness 'cause it'll come with peace side by side. So reach for the door. Open it, and step out. It ain't gon' be easy, cutting those ties. It's gonna hurt like a mother. But that pain? That's the sound of your chains breaking. Listen to it, and savor that music, while you feel that sunlight on your face, and that fresh air in your lungs.

Look in the mirror again, for real this time. See the King, or the Queen the Warrior you were always meant to be. Your vision unclouded. Now go claim your throne. The streets ain't built to hold you down, it's there for you to get to your destination. So be smart and travel hard. You are built to rise. You are built to grow. Even the nature says so. Don't believe me? Look at your baby pictures and then look in the damn mirror. Now bust a move!

The Price of Peace: Reclaiming Your Soul

Yeah like I've mentioned, walking away is gonna hurt like a fresh cut, that initial sting is real. You gonna feel like you leaving a piece of yourself behind, like you cutting off your own damn arm. You gonna second-guess yourself, replay those few good times like they're the whole damn movie, and wonder if you're tripping, if you've made the right call.

But listen, nostalgia's a smooth-talking liar, paints a pretty picture that ain't the whole damn canvas. Memory's an editor, remember that! It cuts out all the BS and leaves you with the highlights, fooling you into believing the lie. You can't blame your brain for doing what it does best, tryna keep you sane. That's just surviving. And there's nothing wrong with you, for painting a pretty picture of the painful moments. You gotta try hard to remember the truth, which will give you more fuel to walk away. That pain of walking away? That's the real price you gotta pay for peace, the cost of getting your soul back, of buying back your freedom. You don't owe nobody a lifetime of chances just 'cause you shared some moments, some laughs, some late-night whispers. You sure as hell don't owe 'em your future just 'cause they're lingering in your past, a phantom limb.

If they really wanted to change, you wouldn't be sitting here confused, dazed, and wondering. Their actions would be screaming the truth louder than any damn words that exist. If they truly valued you, you wouldn't be second guessing your worth, you'd feel it in your bones, undeniable. Time to choose yourself, homie. Time to walk. This is the real sh*t right here. If you stay now, after all the damn signs, after all the pain they dished out? That ain't on them no more. That weight falls squarely on your shoulders for not having the damn grit to walk away. It's you who's avoiding the pain of ripping sh*t up. Feel?

You gotta level up, become that individual who ain't gonna let their soul leak out slow and painful. You gotta become the one who patches it up and walks with determination. Determined to be free and determined to be strong, even when the tears sting your eyes, even when your chest feels like it's been ripped open. Real strength ain't about being emotionless; it's about feeling that damn hurt and still putting one foot in front of the other. Sh*t... thugs don't cry? Don't even play with me fam! Real ones feel, and then they move with emotion as a fuel for success and not destruction.

Keeping The Snakes Out For Good:
The Phoenix Rising

See you're a human being with emotions and there's always gonna be doubt about every decision you've made or question the future moves and that's okay. That's your survival code kicking in. But what's not okay is to step backward by listening to that doubt or get stung by the questions in your dome about what's next, and froze up. After you cut ties with these snakes, their main doorway back into your life is the voices in your head. You gotta learn how to make Boss decisions and stick with them. Gotta burn every damn fu#ked up bridges, every damn escape routes they can use to get back in your head, back in your heart. Silence is the key medicine for a broken heart, a clean break is the only way to truly heal. I'm not talking 'bout locking your self in a room and disconnect from the whole damn world. I'm talking about silence against those that put you down and leaving them no maps to the roads and keys to the doors back into your world. The world you're rebuilding. Remember, you had to rebuild because of them, so torch the memories, the pics, the damn letters and messages – all that noise from a love that was never real, a one-sided dream. Build your life back, brick by damn brick, a new routine that leaves no cracks for their ghost to slip back into.

Replace that wasted time, those hours spent waiting and hoping like a fool, with focus on your grind, your goals, your dreams, your damn purpose. Surround yourself with your day-ones, the real homies and Tru Fam who kept it 💯, who lift you, not let you drown in your own damn tears, the ones that aren't afraid to check you when you starting to go off the road. 'Cause your Tru riders are gon' tell you to kill those damn songs, those spots that bring back their memory, those triggers that send you spiraling. And for the love of all that's Gangsta, stop checking their damn page! Stop looking for some secret message in their posts, some sign that they're missing your sorry ass. Ain't nothing there but air, believe that my people! Stop searching for what ain't existing. They ain't throwing you no damn lifeline. You're just projecting your own wishes 'cause you ain't fully swallowed the bitter pill of reality. Get it done. No half-ways... got me?

And from this day forward, you gotta make a vow to yourself. No more excusing disrespect, no more ignoring inconsistency, no more sacrificing your worth for some fake-ass dream of love. Trust that gut feeling, that voice inside, screaming that something ain't right – nine times outta ten, it's dead on. Stop making excuses for who they could be and face the reality of who they are. The one who traded you broken promises and empty words for your loyalty. You ain't a damn fixer-upper for broken souls. They got programs and real professionals that will handle that, so let them do their job and you live your life like you supposed to live, Free and Happy. You here to grow, to become a solid-ass individual. Anything pulling you off that path ain't love, it's a damn detour, a distraction from your destiny. Detaching is coming back home to yourself, reconnecting with the person you were before the world tried to tell you your worth depended on being chosen.

Choosing Yourself: The Crown Fits

And when you finally get back to that strong-ass self, you gonna realize the truth. You weren't waiting for them to change, you were waiting for **you** to change. For the moment you finally said "enough is enough." For the moment you stopped calling pain love. For the moment you are convinced when you say "I don't need to be chosen, 'cause I choose myself." For the moment you chose clarity over confusion, truth over illusion? That moment is now, my friend. Grab it.

Look at your life passing by. Every day you stay stuck is a day you miss out on your own damn peace and the happiness that comes with it, and your own damn expansion. An OG once told me, straight wisdom from the streets: **'If they ain't adding, they subtracting.' Simple as that. Period!** Life's out there, waiting beyond their limited joy, beyond their fleeting passion, beyond their existence. See, their world? It's just a small corner of this massive universe, filled with their temporary highs and whatever drama they got brewing. But your life, your potential? That stretches way beyond their damn horizon my Kings and Queens. You think your whole world revolves around their limited vision of joy, and their here-to-day-gone-tomorrow flings? Nah, playa, you a star in your own right, and your galaxy is way bigger than their little planet.

Trying to turn these toxic people into the version you desired is like waiting for rain in the desert without any cloud in sight. It's like staring at the same damn door, hoping it magically opens. That door? It's locked, bolted, and probably got a 'keep out' sign you've been ignoring. Wishing ain't gonna make it budge, my Brothas, and Sistas. You gotta understand, some doors are meant to stay closed, and the universe got a funny way of showing us that. So, let some other fools think that they can pick the lock and try it, while you move on to the next better thing.

Spreading Your Wings: The Unfolding Horizon

And the sooner you walk away, the sooner you're gonna see how many other doors are waiting for you to knock, how many new paths are opening up, how many new horizons are revealing themselves. You've been tunnel-visioned on this one dead end, missing the whole damn landscape of possibilities. The moment you turn your back and step away, it's like the fog lifts, and you see a whole city of opportunities you never knew existed. Different vibes, different energies, different journeys waiting for you.

You ain't broken, you breaking out of a damn cage, spreading your wings. You've been trapped in this emotional cell, thinking this was all there was. But now? You busting out, feeling that fresh air on your face for the first time in a long time. Those wings you got? They've been folded up for too damn long, stifled. Time to unfurl 'em and see how high you can fly, how far you can soar.

And that pain you feel right now, that ache in your chest? That ain't the end of your story, that's the jump-start to your rebirth, the fire that's gonna forge you into something stronger, something better, something truly magnificent. Think of it like this: they gotta break down the old building to put up a skyscraper, right? So, this pain? It's the demolition crew tearing down the weak, unstable parts so you can build something solid and magnificent in its place. That ache? That's the heat tempering the steel of your soul, making you resilient, unbreakable, ready for anything.

The Power of Exhalation: Breathe and Conquer

Now, Don't just stand there, feeling sorry for yourself. Take that pain, that newfound clarity, and use it as fuel. Step out of that trash's life. Stop Waiting for them to change up and step into that world that's been waiting for you, yearning for your presence. The only reason why you can't smell the stench of trash is because you're nose-blinded. You've been living with it for so long you can't smell it no more, but guess what? Everyone 'round you can, my Royal kin. So wake up and show 'em what you made of. Show 'em the King, the Queen, you truly are. Leave that closed door in your damn rear-view mirror and never look back. Your future ain't behind you, it's straight ahead.

Here, just in case you in deep sh*t, like they got you real good, I'm gonna break it down for you even further. Check it. It's like this! You ain't just waiting, you're damn near suffocating on what could be, on a phantom future. You see them, this ideal in your mind, but they ain't seeing the crown you holding high. You breathing shallow, hoping they'll just wake up and see the damn Royalty standing right there? That's a trap, my Royal. A gilded cage built on "maybe someday," and on empty promises.

That air you holding in? It's the weight of what ain't happening. It's the anchor dragging you down while they out there living their story, and you stuck on a chapter that ain't writing itself, stuck in a state of suspended animation. You think time gonna magically flip the script? Nah, that's a fairytale for folks who ain't got the grit to grab the pen themselves and write their own damn ending.

Let that breath OUT. Feel the release? That's the first step to reclaiming your lungs, your life force, your sovereignty. You ain't blind, homie. Your eyes are wide open, and you see the truth, even if you trying to blur the edges. They ain't oblivious; they're making choices, I mean conscious choices, and you ain't the one they choosing right now.

So what you gonna do? Keep gasping for air that ain't coming? Keep playing the fool in this one-act play of their design? Hell no!

You got a choice right here, right now. You can stay chained to this phantom hope, or you can break the damn lock. You can keep begging for crumbs of attention, or you can feast at your own table, nourishing your own damn spirit.

Choose Power. That ain't about flexing or fronting. It's about taking control of your own damn narrative. It's about looking in the mirror and seeing the King or Queen you know you are, regardless of who else acknowledges it. It's about moving like a force, not a shadow.

Choose Peace. And that ain't about being soft. It's about silencing the noise of that longing, that doubt, that anxiety. It's about finding your center, your solid ground, so no one can shake you. It's about walking away from the drama and the disrespect with your head held high, knowing your worth ain't up for debate.

Let them live their life. You gotta build yours. Stop holding your breath for a dream that's keeping you from breathing your own damn air. Exhale the past, inhale the future. **Stop Waiting** for them, because Your power and your peace are waiting for you. Go claim 'em. Straight up.

Rule #2: Know Your Damn Value
(The Unbreakable Standard)

Listen up, fam! This ain't up for debate, and definitely not a "maybe" situation. They ain't the damn trophy you gotta win. **YOU are the Got-Damn prize!** You're the one bringing the value, the realness, the uncut truth to the table. Any individual, any situation, any opportunity that can't see that from the jump? It don't deserve access to your kingdom. Period.

From day one, the world been slinging that dope, a script that everyone swallowed hook, line, and sinker. Got 'em all hypnotized. They told you external approval is the ultimate win, that all your hard work, all your victories, don't count 'til someone gives you the damn thumbs up. They made you believe the peak of your game is them choosing your sorry ass outta the lineup. Come on now, why else would you ever feel like you need to compete with another individual? Why else your head be twisted like that? Feeling like you gotta flex harder than your ex's new boo or on a whole another level of messy is when you think you gotta outshine someone that your snake partner is creeping with, instead of just straight up ghosting their sorry ass? That's poison, straight up venom, fam. That sh*t has been infecting generations of good people, leaving 'em empty shells, begging for scraps of attention. Folks are killing each other tryna impress a damn facade. That weak sh*t has been growing bigger and bigger by the day. I'm not saying you ain't gotta be fly. What I'm tryna paint homie, is you gotta be fly for **you**, and not for no damn attention.

Look around you, playa! You see these individuals out here jumping through hoops like Got-Damn trained animals, doing tricks for a quick smile, a second glance from someone who already wrote 'em off in their mind. They putting on a whole damn show for someone who ain't even in the audience for them. What did B.I.G say?

"Straight up, honey, really I'm asking,

Most of these niggas think they be macking,

but they be acting

Who they attracting with that line,

'What's your name? What's your sign?'

Soon as he buy that wine, I just creep up from behind."

They brainwashed you into building this external validation up on some fake-ass pedestal, made of nothing but fool's gold. Worshiping every damn text like it's the holy grail, climbing this never-ending mountain of their demands, hoping that if you just debase yourself enough, show them undying loyalty even when they treat you like dirt, they'll finally thaw out that frozen heart and throw you some weak-ass version of love. Yeah, that's as real as a damn mirage in the desert. And if you're thirsty, playa, sh*t... you are in serious trouble my friend. This trash you're with, they played you, made you think they're some untouchable goddess or a god you gotta pray to for their blessings. Well, grab a damn sledgehammer my Kings and

Queens, 'cause we about to smash those idols they made for you to worship into a million pieces! That whole damn fantasy you been living in? That's been your prison all along, locking you down, keeping you blind to your own damn power. **You the prize, my friend.** Start acting like it. I know you ain't picking up my lines. Come on, G, I'm not gonna let you drown. So, here, here is another line, grab it and hold onto it for your dear life. This line could've even saved Leo in the Titanic. Nah, just playing, people. He was a straight G for that sh*t. Alright, serious mode! Let me break it down to you with some more sauce so you'd really taste the depth and seriousness of the importance of your value. Let my words sink in before you sink in that cold ass ocean of manipulation tactics.

The Gold Medal Mentality: You Are the Championship

Check it, 'cause this line right here is the damn core of it all. **External validation was never the damn finish line you gotta cross. YOU are the gold medal, the damn championship belt.** And until that truth sinks deep into your bones, until it's the air you breathe and the rhythm of your heart, you gonna keep losing yourself in these damn chases, running after people who wouldn't even throw their dirty dish water on you, if you were on fire unless you were holding something they wanted.

Peep this real-life scenario, straight from the streets. My homie, he tried to do me a solid, and threw a bone my way, tried to hook me up with this one baddie – let's call her "Whatever-the-fu*k" 'cause that's how I remembered it. He gave her my digits, but radio silence. Ghosted. Vanished. Now, your boy ain't about to get all bent outta shape about it. 'Cause sh*t... I'm already choosing Power and living it daily, ditching every-damn-thing that doesn't pay me.. ya dig?

Anyway, then outta nowhere, three weeks later, this weak-ass text pops up: "Hey, this is Whatever-the-fu*k. Me and my girlfriend, we stranded out here in Wherever-the-fu*k. You wanna be a 'nice guy' and call us an Uber?" My response? Froze her ass out, fam. "Aw damn, that's a shame! Nah, nice guys finish last." You know what her comeback was? ":(". A damn emoji! This was a certified baddie, rolling with a whole crew of other baddies. I've seen the flicks. But see, **knowledge? That's the damn antidote to the poison of illusions.** I ain't falling for that weak play. It's a Boss move to help out, no doubt. And I would've done it if she asked straight up with no lies and some explanations.

The power I felt in that moment, homie? That's the juice I want you to taste. I wasn't being straight-up disrespectful, I was speaking the damn truth. Think about it. she had all that time to hit me up, just a simple "hey," but she didn't. And when she finally slid into my DMs, it's 'cause she needed a favor and didn't even ask me properly? Get the hell outta here with that weak-ass hustle. Turns out, she and one of her "boy-toys" were the ones stranded, and she probably figured playing the damsel in distressed with another chick would make me more likely to play the damn hero.

That moment, homie, that's what it feels like to value yourself. To know that you ain't no Uber calling, yes ma'am-ing, the word

'Sucka' and 'Punk' tatted on the forehead pushover. Especially for no dusty individuals who couldn't be bothered to acknowledge your existence until they needed something. That's the power of knowing that **you're the prize.** You ain't a damn option, you're the main event. Start treating yourself like one. When you choose your own damn power, fam, your gut, that inner voice, is always gonna guide you to success. Trust!

See, that feeling deep down in your core? That ain't just indigestion, that's your internal GPS system, always pointing you towards what's real and what's right for your damn journey. When you start moving based on your own strength, that voice gets louder, it gets clearer, and it'll steer you straight through the bullsh*t and right to your wins. Doubt that feeling? You gonna end up lost in the damn deserts, chasing mirages, and dying alone. No one will remember your name, not even their trashy asses.

"If you believe, you must achieve. if you doubt, you'll go without."

The Tru Measure of a Royal: Unyielding Standards

A real individual's worth ain't measured by how much you bend over backwards, how much you sacrifice your own well-being to win over someone who barely acknowledges your existence. Nah, playa. That's the game of a fool, thinking you gotta diminish yourself to be worthy of someone else's attention. A real individual's value? It shines through how fiercely you protect your **standards** – those ain't just suggestions, they're the rules of your kingdom. It's about guarding your precious **energy** – that's your life force, you ain't gon' be leaking it on someone who don't appreciate a single drop. It's about your life's **purpose** – that's your damn mission on this earth, and you ain't gon' let nobody derail you from that trail that you're blazing, period! And your limited **time** – that's the most valuable currency you got, you ain't gon' waste it on dead ends.

Words are powerful, homie, so check this before you start hating on anyone, 'cause that ain't what this about. Sure, some folks can be ruthless but don't fall for the trend and think for yourself. Don't become one of those people that just say sh*t, 'cause it sounds good. That's just your pain talking. Some individuals ain't the villains for valuing others differently. They wired by nature to seek out the highest value in their orbit. That's just the way it is, the primal code, and you can't fight against the tide of nature. You might as well try to argue with the damn sunrise for shining on your ass on one of those beautiful summer mornings. All I'm saying is if you act like your worth hangs on how much suffering you're willing to endure for their approval, you automatically broadcasting to them that you don't really believe you got any damn value yourself. Even though some people might tolerate that or even love it at first, but eventually their primal code's 'gon kick in and start treating you differently and that toleration and adoration period is gonna expire. That's 'cause you showing that you're insecure and you're afraid to lose them so you're willing to stick around even if they slap you in the face. Ya dig? You putting a discount tag on your own damn soul. And in this cold-blooded game of attraction, they gonna react accordingly: by pulling back like you got the damn COVID, disrespecting your ass like you ain't even a threat, dismissing your efforts like they're just dust in the wind, or straight-up replacing your drunk ass with someone who knows their damn worth and ain't afraid to show it. That's the truth, served cold. So, don't be complaining to your crew that your foot's been hurting 'cause of them, when you the one tryna impress them by walking barefoot for miles, and when you're the one showing them that they can just ignore your problems.

Building Your Fortress: An Impenetrable Kingdom

You gotta evolve into the individual, whose presence is a damn privilege, not some charity handout. You ain't out here begging for scraps, you serving up a damn feast. The individual so locked in on their own growth – constantly leveling up, mentally, physically, spiritually, and of course financially! Their own life mission – laser-focused on their goals, ain't got time for distractions. Their own personal code of conduct – lives by their principles, ain't swayed by the whims of others. For that individual, the very thought of begging for emotional scraps is not just weak, it's a damn joke, a concept so foreign it don't even register. You gotta build your life like a damn fortress, homie. Solid foundation built on self-respect, independent operation, you're running your own damn show, self-governed, making your own rules, your own decisions. They either add to that empire you building, bring something valuable to the table, or they get shown the damn gates, no exceptions. No back stage passes just 'cause they're appealing. It's cool to be an apprentice for a period, but don't let that be your end goal.

Stop chasing after those who give you the cold shoulder, who treat you like you ain't even there. That's like chasing your own damn shadow – pointless and a waste of energy. Start chasing your own greatness with a hunger that can't be satisfied and a thirst that can't be quenched. Let that drive consume you, push you to be better every damn day. So your very existence radiates a force field, a powerful aura that they can feel in their gut before you even utter a damn word. That confidence, that self-respect? That's magnetic. You're letting them know that you ain't gonna be their entertainment, and they need to step up and take you seriously.

How the hell you do that, you asked? Well, first and foremost, you master your own **mind**. That's the battlefield where all your wins and losses are decided. You reprogram yourself daily with the knowledge you soak up from the books you devour – feed your body and brain that good, healthy stuff. The wisdom you gain from the mentors you listen to – find those OG's who been through hell, kicked the devil's balls and came out stronger. The damn crew you roll with – make sure they winners, not whiners. And if your current crew is all about that weak, pity-party bullsh*t? Cut 'em loose, fam! They anchoring your progress. You done docking, it's time to sail to the horizons of success. No more endless scrolling through their social media, asking their people about them, hoping to catch a glimpse of your sorry self in their story. That's just picking at a damn scab, preventing it from healing. No more precious brain space wasted on what they're doing or who they're hanging with. That's their damn movie, remember that they had you in there as a back up. Now you the star of your own. You gotta throw all that wasted energy into being a King or a Queen of action – get off your ass and bust a move, stay disciplined – stick to your damn plan. Learn from your mistakes and the mistakes of others, and pursue real wealth – in all its forms: financial, emotional, and spiritual. Don't aim to be the person who's getting pay checks, but aim to become the one who signs the damn paychecks.

Non-Negotiables and Real Wealth: Your Unbreakable Decree

You gotta set anything that you feel, which are non-negotiables in stone. **No more chasing!** You the prize, remember? **No more waiting 'round like a damn puppy** – your time is valuable. **No more dealing with any form of disrespect** – your boundaries are sacred. And absolutely **no more chances** for folks who showed you their Tru colors – believe what they show you, especially over and over again. You gotta get brutally honest with yourself. Look in the mirror and tell yourself the truth, no sugarcoating. If they ain't investing in you – time, effort, and genuine care. If they ain't coming at you with the same damn fire you got for them, or even a bigger and brighter one? Then they ain't the one. Plain and simple! And clinging to them ain't loyalty, it's straight-up self-betrayal. So, show some respect to yourself and level up your damn frame, 'cause a strong-ass body screams a strong-ass mind. You ain't out here looking soft, projecting that weak sh*t into your hustle wondering why your ass is broke. You build that temple, carve that physique, 'cause it shows you got discipline, you got that dog in you, you conquering your damn demons. That ain't just 'bout looking like a Boss, it's 'bout feeling like a damn Conquerer inside and out and handling your business. You handle your own paper, 'cause real freedom ain't 'bout depending on nobody else's handouts, begging for nickels and dimes. It's 'bout being your own shot-caller, running your own crew, building your own empire so you ain't under anyone's control. You cultivate your purpose so deep and meaningful that your value shoots through the roof, while theirs, if they chose to front on your existence, becomes straight-up irrelevant to your grind. You got your own mountain to conquer, your own fate to carve. Let some other clueless marks, the ones too green to know better or too stubborn to wise up, refused to pick up this book, and pick up their slack instead. They can chase that mirage. You got real Got-Damn power moves to make.

The Gravitational Pull of Self-Respect: A New Orbit

Stop your sniffling over people who ghosted your ass when you were right there, offering your realness, your uncut truth. You laid your heart on the line, showed 'em the real you, and they bounced? Oh well... Their loss. Not yours. Feel me? You gotta become so untouchable to that weak-ass energy, that maybe one day when you vibing with people, only the truest, most genuine souls even catch a glimpse of your locked-in focus. You ain't wasting your precious time on no subtraction pretending to be an attraction. Right?

Let me break it down again so you'd understand this street knowledge. A real G ain't just 'bout stacking sh*t and running sh*t. It's 'bout that quiet, ice-cold confidence that screams, 'I'm in control of my own life!' You know your worth down to your soul. And if they can't clock that truth, that's their blindness, not your problem. It's 'bout rolling out with style, with your head held high the second they hesitate, the second they show you any doubt, the second they show you Tru disrespect. You ain't begging for no damn love. It's 'bout being so damn solid and self-made on your own that their absence don't even cause a ripple in your game. Your happiness ain't chained to nobody else's shadow.

And you gotta live this damn code, not just moving your lips and flowing like a smooth talker. You gotta bleed it, breathe it, and you gotta live it every single day. These streets got eyes and ears you ain't never even dreamed of. These folks got a sixth sense for fakes. They can smell a poser quicker than a rat sniffs out cheese. You can't fake this realness, 'cause these parasites are naturally wired to sniff out a phony from miles away. Why? 'Cause that's how they survive. They're the ones looking in that cracked up dirty ass mirror everyday, learning the game inside and out. Their reflection is their best teacher. They got a super radar for when someone's just flossing versus when they're a stand-up G with real self-respect. And a stand up G, with that unbreakable self-respect? That's their Kryptonite. 'Cause these G's are not hopeless, they're not desperate. These snakes can smell desperation like a bloodhound on a scent. Desperation? Now, that's chum in the water. They're hungry for that weakness. But When you flip the script, from seeing them as the jackpot to knowing that you are the Got-Damn prize, **you become the damn earthquake, The shining Sun. The sun that ain't begging for it's light to shine on the mountains that aren't moving.** You stop fearing loss and start carefully choosing partners who actually bring something valuable to your already fulfilled life. You ain't looking for no charity case to complete your already progressing and prospering empire. You're simply welcoming the one who will help increase it like a Boss that you are. No subtractions unless it's toxic!

Operating from Abundance: Your World, Your Rules

Real moves on the streets? You wake up early and own your block before anyone else even rolls outta bed. You ain't laying around waiting for them to call the damn shots. You master a skill or trade like your whole life depends on it. 'Cause it does! You build something concrete, something that leaves a legacy. You handle every conversation, every meet-up knowing damn well that you're the one doing the surveying, not the other way around. You ain't auditioning for no role. You stop over-explaining your moves, stop fighting for a spot in nobody's life. Like I've said before, if they blind to your shine, that's their problem. And you sure as hell stop accepting the bare minimum as anything but a straight-up diss. You deserve the top shelf, so demand that respect after you're built like that. 'Cause you work hard for that sh*t! You build your side hustles, your passions, and your tight-knit crew outside of romantic pursuits, so your emotional well-being ain't never at the mercy of their mood swings. Your peace comes from your own damn hustle, not from begging to scandalous snakes, when they finally bless you with a chump change. You cultivate that cold, calm detachment that silently screams, 'I want you in my world, but I damn sure don't need you to help me breathe. If you ride with me, you elevate my game. If you bounce, you ain't taking nothing away from me! Not-ta-Damn-Nada!' That's the real power right there. And by living like that, you become ten times more attractive, not just to potential partners, but to the whole damn world, 'cause real abundance flows to those who ain't desperately reaching for it. People respect a G who stands on their own two. By doing that, you may even offend some, but secretly those who are offended are wishing they got the heart to do what you do, and how you move. Trust! That's 'cause you learn valuable lessons from every damn back-stabs without letting bitterness turn your heart.

You ain't carrying that damn weight. Every act of disrespect against you is a motive to build your walls even stronger, so that you don't ever let the snakes back into your kingdom. You gotta handle disrespect like a real G. I'm talking a real disrespect with solid proof that's built on real evidence and not no assumptions, 'cause petty arguments and actions based on assumptions are for the Simps not no Bosses. What I mean by handling it like a real G is that, you ain't bitter sitting there wasting your time plotting for their downfalls or hoping some bad sh*t happen to the ones that hurt you. So, You just move on by taking that pain as a gift. A gift of fuel for your success, feel me? Like I mentioned before, time is valuable. Fool me once, forget you, but thank you for the lesson and the fuel. And you use that fuel and move through this life with a fire in your chest that no rejection can ever put out. Your inner flame burns strong regardless of the damn noises. A real G ain't about throwing hands at every little jab. That's small-time energy. We talking chess moves, not checkers. When disrespect comes knocking, a Tru Royalty handles it with a different kind of power – the power of intellect and unwavering self-respect.

Think about it: you're building an empire, stacking that paper, chasing that next level. Why let some petty beef derail your whole damn train? You're now operating from abundance. A clever G sees disrespect for what it is: usually someone else's insecurity or attempt to knock you off your square. Reacting with violence just validates their noise and drags you down to their level.

Instead, a real one is gonna:

* Ice 'em out with silence: Sometimes, the coldest burn is no reaction at all. It shows their words ain't got no weight, no power over you. It's like they throwing rocks at a fortress – ain't nothing moving.

* Hit 'em with the unexpected class: Respond with calm, maybe even a slight smile. It throws 'em off balance 'cause they're expecting a fight. It shows you operate on a different plane.

* Use words like a surgeon's scalpel: A sharp, well-placed remark can cut deeper than any punch, expose their weakness without getting your hands dirty. It's about intellect over impulse.

* Turn it into motivation: Use the disrespect as fuel. Let it drive you to grind harder, prove 'em wrong with your success. Living well is the best revenge, and a G knows that paper talks louder than fists.

* Strategically address it if needed: If the disrespect is a real threat to your reputation or business, a smart G will handle it strategically. Maybe a quiet word behind closed doors, a calculated move that asserts dominance without unnecessary bloodshed. It's about protecting your assets and your name.

At the end of the day, a real one knows their worth. They ain't gotta prove it by beating down every fool that mouths off. Their focus is on building, and on leveling up. They understand that Tru power ain't in the muscle, it's in the mind and the hustle. They're too busy counting stacks to be worried about petty squabbles. That's how a real one handles disrespect – with intelligence, class, and also with unwavering focus on the bigger picture. Remember that you wear your crown on your head not in your hands. But sometimes you just have no other option but to take that crown off and humble'em with it, and teach'em, feel? That should always be your last and final option 'cause you're now build like a Boss, a real G, a Tru Royalty.

When you finally stop treating others like goddesses or gods dropping from the heavens to bless your unworthy ass with their precious time, and you start seeing your own self as the rare, high-value Boss you were always meant to be, every damn thing flips. Not 'cause others magically change, but 'cause you finally stopped handing over your crown to someone who could never truly hold it for you. If your own neck ain't strong enough to rock that crown, homie, how the hell is anybody else gonna recognize that you are, in fact, a damn King or a Queen? **You gotta wear that crown with pride,** and I do mean pride not arrogance. Trust me, there's a difference. And if you're gonna choose power and peace, you got to know the difference between pride and arrogance. Pride is truly living on your hard works, and giving back to your community and arrogance is living on credit and blinding people on purpose, 'cause your insecure ass is shining under borrowed light for minute. When you operating from abundance, you're gonna shine by a Tru light source that ain't never going out, trust!

The Unbreakable Decree: Claim Your Truth

In relationships, you stop investing in the fantasy of 'what could be' and start demanding concrete proof: consistent effort, unwavering loyalty, genuine respect – not just sweet damn nothings but actions that speak louder than any damn promises. Show your hands, don't just run your mouth. In friendships, you ruthlessly ditch anyone who's draining your ambition instead of fueling your fire. Ain't got time for no leeches. I'm not saying not to throw your day-ones some knowledge on getting their head right, in fact you should put them young bucks and the OG's on game if they are straying, but what I am saying is after you've done all that you can without compromising your growth and if they ain't picking up what you're laying down, then it's time to ghost, homie. You only get one life, so do what's best for your conscience. Whether you're physically locked up or walking free, time is your most valuable damn asset; invest it wisely. In life, you operate from a place of genuine abundance. If one door slams shut, another one will pop open, long as you keep sharpening your blade. Keep leveling up your game. If they betray your trust, don't worry! It's better to find out sooner then later and plus, better, more solid alliances are waiting down the block. The streets respect loyalty. If anyone doubt your potential, their opinion is just background noise under the march of your destiny with individuals who are Tru damn Kings and Queens. (Damnnn, that's a quotable line right there! Can someone please spray that sh*t on a wall!)

You ain't no satellite orbiting someone else's world. **You the damn planet.** Build your own gravitational pull, the one you can control. A control so strong that anything that ain't real just gets flung off into space. Stop worshiping at the temple of temporary. Your worth ain't measured in the glances you catch or the numbers you dial. It's built brick by damn brick inside you. Your mind? That's your Tru kingdom. Fortify it with knowledge, discipline, and self-respect. Let peace be your damn general, guarding the gates against any B.S that tries to creep in. You wanna detach from somebody who can't see your value? Don't waste your breath on hate or petty shots. Elevate. Ascend. Outgrow their whole damn perspective until their noise just fades into silence. That's how You operate on a different level, a clear frequency, and a higher vibration.

And when you do that? You ain't just free from them. You snapping every damn chain you ever shackled yourself with, chasing after shadows. Forget who you were told you are, or crying 'bout the hand you were dealt. That's yesterday's news. Today, you claim your birthright: genuine security, shatterproof happiness. That ain't a damn wish; it's a Got-Damn decree. Feel that in your bones, homie. 'Cause that's your truth, so claim it!

Rule #3: Walk Away Smooth (W.A.S.)

W.A.S. That's past tense, fam. So leave the past where it belongs, 'cause this is the damn point of no return. The final word on cutting ties and reclaiming your soul again. Let's inject this with that pure, uncut street sh*t, that gangster finality that leaves no room for doubt. You ready to slam the door shut for good? Bye Felicia…

Sever. Every. Single. Damn. Connection.

You gotta combine every rule you learned so far to make this sh*t happen. Think about it, you still got a thread, a string, a digital leash tied to their world in any damn way? That's like leaving the vault door wide open after you finally cleaned out the thieves. They still got a key, a code, a damn back alley into your mind. That's an invitation for the storm to roll back in and tear your life apart again. They still got a foothold, an anchor sunk deep into your soul, holding you down in their toxic ocean. The real glow-up, the Tru damn mending of your broken spirit, demands a clean break, a surgical cut.

Go ghost, vanish like a phantom in the night. Complete radio silence. No weak-ass explanations, no farewell tours, no lingering glances back like a damn Simp yearning for scraps. Just a decisive fade into your own destiny, like a Boss moving on to bigger and better empires.

And let's be crystal clear, aight? This ain't no petty-ass tactic to make them suddenly wake up and realize the Royal they lost. You ain't playing no games with that person's weak-ass mind. This is about you finally seeing your own damn worth, the **uncut diamond** you've been letting dust cover up that shine.

So let me remind you of what (I hope) you have soaked up so far. **Rule #1: Stop Waiting** for that trash to magically change. That's wasted energy, a damn fool's errand. **Rule #2: Know Your Damn Value You think they're the jackpot you gotta win back? Hell to the damn no, playa. YOU are that Triple 7s.** You're the **Masterpeace** in progress, the uncut gem that shines brighter than any damn fool's gold. If you've soaked up those rules then you are finally ready for **Rule #3: W.A.S Walk Away Smooth. This act of cutting every tie, every route that'll take you straight back to them? That's the ultimate power move, a declaration of self-respect etched in stone, written in your own blood.** It's drawing that unbreakable line in the concrete: on one side, the weak version of you who endured the stupid drama, who let their chaos steal your peace of mind. On the other side? The emergence of a stronger, more self-aware you, a warrior who ain't tolerating that bullsh*t no more. So, let's put this sh*t in motion.

The Death Trap of Digital Ghosts

I know I've mentioned it before but I gotta say it again, because this is the death trap where so many playas get caught, stuck in the emotional quicksand, drowning in their own tears. They tap that delete button on their phone, feeling like they just conquered the world, but their "master's" ghost still whispers their name in old photos they refused to throw away, haunting their memories. They halt the texts, but their thumbs still twitch like a crackhead, hovering over their "master's" social media, becoming digital stalkers haunting their online presence. They might block them on one platform, puffing out their chest with a fake-ass sense of victory, only to be lurking on another damn app, feeding their weak obsession like a fiend jonesing for a fix. That ain't detachment. Trust! That's just a slightly less direct view of the same entanglement, the same damn chains holding them down in the same damn prison. The prison these "masters" made special for them Simps. Thinking they've escaped the cage by changing rooms, but it's just a different cell, and with a different window.

Yo, you still looking lost in the maze, like a rookie on their first night? Let me shine another streetlamp on this whole situation so you can finally see the corners. I'm gonna carve this truth into your understanding one more time, so it ain't just some whisper in the alley, I want this etched in your damn soul like a clean ass tag on a brick wall. Feel?

Let me paint you a vivid picture. As long as they occupy any space in your reality, even if it's just their digital crumbs on your screen, you're still locked in chains, homie. Think of your mind like your turf, your personal hood. Every time you let their digital ghost linger on your screen, it's like letting a rat set up shop in your prime crib. They ain't paying no rent, they just causing static and taking up valuable head-space. Every time your eyes drift over to their profile, every brainless scroll through their feed, you out there watering dead-ass flowers in the graveyard of your busted-ass past. You trying to resurrect something that's deader than one of Pharaoh's dudes Moses smoked. You wasting your precious time and energy on a corpse. You fueling that illusion in your head that things could somehow rewind, that maybe, just maybe, they'll have some damn epiphany. You think that person gonna magically wake up one morning and realize what a fool they have been? That's a straight-up pipe dream, my friend. You chasing a ghost that ain't never gonna materialize. And every time your ass caves and responds to that half-hearted "how you doing?" text, that breadcrumb they throw your way like you're some pigeon? You handing them the damn remote control to your emotions. You letting them play your feelings like a cheap-ass arcade game, and providing all the quarters. You teaching them they can get a free ride to your energy, suck up your attention without offering one ounce of real commitment. You showing them that you're a welcome mat they can wipe their dusty-ass feet on, whenever they come home after kicking it with them bums.

Cleansing Your Kingdom: Eliminating the Parasites

This ain't just confined to no busted-ass romance. Hell to the damn no, this infection spreads like a plague way beyond that heartbreak. These **emotional vampires, these soul-sucking leeches**, they come creeping in all sorts of disguises, blending in like creepy ass chameleons. They could be them fake-ass "friends" who thrive on your drama, injecting their poison into your peace like a serpent striking. They ain't fixing your broke game; they dragging your ass down to their level. They could even be them toxic-ass damn co-workers or neighbors who cross every line and smile in your face while they stab you in the back. The bottom line, fam, the unshakable damn truth, the code of the streets? **Cut. All. Contacts. Across the whole board, no exceptions.** How are you supposed to grow with all that unhealthy weight on you? You can't help picking anyone up when your ass is the one on the ground. You gotta sever every damn tie, burn every damn bridge to the ground that can lead back to them, and build a fortress around your soul so high they can't even see a sky when they stand next to it. Cleanse your life from these emotional parasites if you ever wanna breathe free again and reclaim your peace, your sanity. You gotta protect your energy like it's the last thing you got in this cold-ass world.

Silence isn't just the absence of noise; it's a fortress. Distance isn't avoidance; it's armor. Embrace the solitude. In this decisive act of separation, say: 'I Choose Power. I choose my well-being. I choose my future, unburdened by the ghosts of the past.'

Walking away from that poison tree you were tangled up in? That ain't no punk move. Feel? That's straight-up **Boss level**. You were caught in a web, sticky and draining, each day a hustle just to breathe. But you ain't no fly caught in amber. You felt that grip tightening, that venom seeping, and you made a play.

Think of it like this: that relationship was a busted-ass whip, all flash and pain. You were the workhorse, pulling that dead weight, gaining nothing but bruises. Every argument, every lie, every time you had to swallow your pride? That was another lash mark on your soul. But a Tru Royal knows when to ditch the broken ride. You saw the engine was shot, the wheels were wobbling, and that destination was straight-down to hell. So you hopped out, dusted off your shoulders, and kept it moving.

Ripping that bandage off? Man, that ain't a gentle peel. That's a swift, hard yank. You felt that sting, that raw ache of what was, but underneath? Fresh skin, ready to breathe. You ain't gotta keep picking at that scab, reopening old wounds. That chapter's closed, homie, the book's on the shelf. Matter fact, put that in the trash where it belongs, and replace it with this Antidote.

Being a strong person ain't about flexing muscles and catching ones. It's about knowing your worth, recognizing when something's toxic, and having the stones to walk away clean. You ain't gotta explain it, ain't gotta beg for understanding. You made your choice, silent and solid. That's the quiet power of a Tru don. You just leveled up, homie, leaving the weak sh*t behind. Now you're striding on your own two, the air is clearer, and the road ahead? It's yours to pave. Remember that.

Wisdom from the Streets: Lessons from the OGs

If you don't wanna listen to me, then check these OGs, and don't you even say 'Well Sunny, they all dead.' That's not the damn point. And that just straight disrespectful, SO CHECK IT!

Tupac Shakur: "Death is not the greatest loss in life. The greatest loss is what dies inside of us while we live." (You can't keep letting people walk all over you, homie. That will kill what's inside of you while you're still breathing. Get eaten alive by parasites is worse than death. Ya dig?)

The Notorious B.I.G.: "It's like the more money we come across, the more problem we see." (Sometimes, the more you try to hold on to what seems attractive to the eyes, the more dramas it brings.)

El-Hajj Malik el-Shabazz (Malcolm X): "You can't separate peace from freedom, because no one can be at peace unless he has his freedom." (Cutting those ties is about freeing yourself, and reclaiming your peace.)

Let's stack some real gangster sh*t right here—bars of wisdom that hit like a .44 but uplift like prayers in the trenches. Ponder upon these points.

- **"Pain is tuition in the school of growth**—don't waste the lesson." Every tear, every betrayal, every sleepless night? That's payment. You already paid the price, so don't walk away empty-handed. Graduate with wisdom or stay repeating the same damn class. The choice is yours.
- **"You can't heal in the same environment that made you bleed."** Trying to grow in a toxic space is like planting roses in concrete soaked in gasoline. Step out the fire before you become ashes in someone else's chaos.
- **"Stop making homes in people who treat you like a hotel."** Temporary comfort ain't worth permanent scars. If they check in and out of your life like it's nothing, why you laying down roots there?
- **"Don't become a Royal who forgets their worth and becomes a jester in their own court."** Don't entertain the disrespect just to feel seen. You weren't born to dance for crumbs. You were built to rule—act like it.
- **"Loyalty to the wrong one is treason to yourself."** Being real don't mean being blind. Don't stay solid in a space where they playing you soft. That ain't loyalty, that's self-betrayal.
- **"You ain't hard for holding on—you're hard when you let go with grace."** Anybody can stay and suffer. But only the strongest walk away in silence, with peace in their pocket and dignity draped like a bulletproof vest.

- **"Some people ain't your future—they're just the storm before your glow-up."** Let 'em pass. They were never meant to stay, only meant to wake you up and shake your soul so you remember who the hell you are.
- **"Real elevation requires isolation."** Ain't no growth when you always surrounded by noise. Sometimes the silence is the gym where your soul lifts the heaviest weight—your past.
- **"Don't chase closure—chase clarity."** Closure is a trap. You don't need their apology to heal. You just need truth, and the truth is: they showed you who they are. That's your exit sign, not a pause button.
- **"Some bonds gotta be broken so your blessings can breathe."** God ain't sending miracles to a mailbox still full of drama. Clear that space. Let peace have a place to land.
- **"Every 'L' you took was just life teaching in disguise. That ain't loss, that's blueprint."** You didn't fail—you learned. You didn't lose—you leveled up. Now build your empire with bricks made from your setbacks.
- **"Never dim your light for someone who can't handle the heat you bring."** If your shine makes them uncomfortable, that's their shadow problem—not your flame. Burn brighter. Burn real.
- **"Cutting someone off ain't hate—it's self-respect with scissors."** You ain't petty. You ain't cruel. You just finally loving yourself enough to protect your peace like it's sacred.
- **"Don't feed people who bite your hand, then ask you what's for dinner."** Starve the snakes. Bless the loyal. And never confuse a smile with sincerity.

- **"You ain't just walking away—you walking towards something greater."** That exit ain't an ending. It's the intro to a new chapter where you run the plot, call the shots, and finally thrive.

The Exit of a Real One (W.A.S.)

W = Withdraw Without Warning. You ever seen a lion announce its exit from the jungle? Hell no. It just disappears, and the silence left behind is loud enough to shake the trees. That's how a real G moves—no warnings, no speeches, just vanishing like smoke when the fire's done burning. You ain't gotta explain why you left that broken table. You ain't required to write a damn essay for people who couldn't even read your pain when it was written across your eyes. **Withdraw without warning** means your peace is no longer up for discussion. You ghost them like they ghosted your worth. You ain't a notification—you're a blackout. Leave 'em wondering. Let 'em ask questions. Let the silence haunt them louder than any word you could've said. 'Cause the real closure ain't in conversation—it's in elevation. Your absence is your answer. Let that sink in.

A = Assert Your Authority. Now that you gone, don't just sit still. Stand the hell up. It's time you **assert your authority** over your own damn life like a warlord taking back their city after the rats had their run. Ain't no more second chances for folks who had VIP access and still treated you like a doormat. This your rebirth, homie. You ain't just walking away—you reclaiming your crown, your peace, and your power. You done renting out your soul for temporary comfort. You the landlord of your energy now, and the rent just went up. If they can't pay with respect, they can't stay. Let 'em talk. Let 'em spin stories. You know the truth, and real ones don't explain themselves to clowns. You ain't bitter—you just done. You ain't angry—you just aware. And awareness is the first step to becoming unbreakable. You ain't soft for leaving. You strong for surviving. You wise for not going back. Ain't no loyalty in drowning with someone who poked holes in the boat.

S = Slide Like a Shadow, Shine Like a Royal. Smooth, not sloppy. Silent, not scared. You **slide out that situation** like a phantom on a mission, leaving no traces but the echo of your last breath in their chaos. Let them figure it out. You already on to your next level. When you slide, you don't stumble. You glide. You walk outta hell like you were just there for sight seeing and you keep it Cool, Calm, and Collected. You don't rush to prove nothing to nobody. Why? 'Cause your growth gonna scream for you louder than your words ever could. And then? You shine. Not for revenge, not for flex—but for you. Your glow-up is sacred. It's divine. It's the result of choosing your damn self for once. You start stacking peace like bricks. You build an empire on boundaries. You become the person you were too distracted to meet. Now when they look up, they don't see the broken version they manipulated. They see a monument of resilience, tall, unshakable, untouchable. They see their Kryptonite. They can't reach you 'cause you ain't on the same level anymore. You ascended. You leveled up, and they still playing tag in the sandbox of their own drama, so you leave them be.

The W.A.S. Mentality

Let this be more than a moment. Let it be your doctrine. When you walk away smooth, you don't just end something—you begin everything. You become a new breed: a person who knows their value, protects their peace, and cuts off anything that threatens either of those.

And if you ever feel tempted to go back, remind yourself:

- **W.A.S. = That's the past, homie.** You ain't gotta return to the scene of the crime just 'cause your heart got soft.
- **W.A.S. = "That was me… but I evolved."** You ain't that version no more.
- **W.A.S. = "Wasted. All. Strength."** 'Cause that's what going back would be.

Remember, healing ain't about staying angry and getting revenge. It's about staying gone for your growth.

Final Street Code: Don't be the one still explaining while they're entertaining. Don't be the one still loving while they're lying. Don't be the one still hoping while they're still joking. Be the one walking away smooth, with your head high, your heart intact, and your future in your hands. And if anyone ever doubts your strength? Just smile and say: "I didn't just walk away—I walked into my damn purpose."

Loved Wrong, Left Right

Celeste wasn't soft — but she had a soft heart. And in the hands of the wrong man, that was like giving a matchbook to an arsonist.

She moved through life like poetry in motion — the kind of woman who remembered your coffee order, who prayed for people behind their backs, who believed that love, if real, was worth the fight.

But then came **Rico**.

He was charming in all the wrong ways — smooth talk, slick smile, the kind of man who could make broken promises sound like lullabies. He walked into Celeste's world with sweet words and slow hands, and before she could blink, he had her orbiting around him like he was the sun.

At first, it felt like love. Or maybe a close counterfeit.

He'd pop in, light up her phone, take her out, talk dreams and loyalty… and then disappear. For days. Sometimes weeks. You know, on that push-pull real player type sh!t.

He always came back with some well-polished excuse.

"I was handling business. You know how it is, baby. I gotta move different."

"My phone been acting up—service out, battery dead, you know how that goes."

"I had to fall back for a minute—too much heat around me. I ain't tryna bring you into that."

"I just needed to clear my head. Everything been moving too fast."

"I ain't wanna hit you until I had something real to show for all this grinding."

"I ain't ghost you—I was just giving you space. You seemed like you needed it."

She wanted to believe him — because believing meant she didn't have to face the truth.

But the thing is truth doesn't stay quiet forever.

Rule #1: Stop Waiting

It started with the waiting. Always waiting.
Waiting for a text back.
Waiting for him to show up when he said he would.
Waiting for his stories to finally match his actions.

There were nights when she'd make his favorite meal, candles lit, hair done — and the food would go cold before her hope did. He wouldn't show, wouldn't call, and somehow she'd still defend him to herself.

"He's just going through something. He'll come around."

That's how it starts — one excuse, after another. Before long, she wasn't living her life — she was living around his absence.

Lena, her best friend, had enough.

"Girl, why you clocking time for a man who don't even check in? You acting like he got potential, but all he got is patterns. You deserve more than this."

Celeste looked down. Her silence was louder than any argument.

"You waiting on a man who disappears every time life gets too real. That ain't love, sis. That's a vanishing act."

But Celeste couldn't pull herself out — not yet. She was still clutching onto those tiny glimpses of who Rico *pretended* to be. It's crazy how long someone can hold onto "maybe."

But even illusions have expiration dates.

Rule #2: Know Your Damn Value

The moment that changed everything came quiet — like betrayal always does.

Celeste had just left the corner store, brown bag in hand, walking home with her hood up. It was late. Wind biting her face. Heart a little heavy, but still hoping — foolishly, maybe — that love could still turn this thing around.

She turned down the shortcut near Maple and 5th. Same alley she'd walked a hundred times. But tonight, something stopped her cold.

A voice. Low, cocky. Laughing in between words.

Rico.

She leaned closer, staying in the shadows.

"Nah, she ain't got a clue. I just keep her feeling important so I can move how I need to. That girl ain't nothing but a soft spot to land. Easy to keep in check."

Then — a second voice. One she hadn't heard in months, but would never forget.

Shayla.

Celeste's heart dropped.

"Keep her distracted. You know how this game go. Let her hold you down while we stack up. When the drop's done, we vanish."

That voice slithered out of the dark like poison, familiar and sharp. It was *her*. Her old homegirl. The one she used to braid hair with on Sundays. The one who came crying after breakups and crashing on couches when life got too real. They'd shared secrets, dreams… loyalty. At least, Celeste had.

But Shayla had vanished months ago — ghosted like she always did when money got tight or a new hustle came around. Celeste never asked why. Never pressed. Just let it be.

Now here she was — posted in an alley with the man Celeste had loved, plotting like her heart wasn't real. Like her kindness was a game to be played.

Celeste stood in that shadow like the air had been knocked clean out her lungs.

Her hands shook. Her mind spun. Her soul snapped back into itself.

And somewhere between rage and heartbreak, a new thought bloomed:

"I ain't nobody's soft spot. I'm the whole foundation."

She walked home that night in silence. Didn't even cry. Not yet.

She sat down in front of her mirror, brown bag still unopened on the table. No music. No TV. Just her reflection.

No makeup. No filter. Just truth.

She stared at herself—really looked. At the tired eyes. The heavy heart. The woman who gave without hesitation. The woman who bent over backwards for people who only showed up when it benefited them.

And suddenly it hit her—**Rico didn't break her.**

She'd been breaking herself… to keep him comfortable.

All those times she stayed silent when her gut told her *something ain't right*. All those nights she loaned love like it was credit he never intended to pay back. All those moments she let *both of them* play in her face.

That's when Rule #2: **Know Your Damn Value** cracked her wide open.

She thought about the car rides, the money she loaned, the stress she carried like it was hers to bear. The fake apologies. The missing hours. The gaslighting.

And through all of that — *she showed up.*

Over. And over. And over.

But the thing is — a woman can only betray herself for so long before something inside her screams, **"No more."**

That night, she didn't text him. She didn't argue. She didn't even block him.

She made a list.

Of everything she gave. Everything she tolerated. Every red flag she painted white.

Not out of bitterness — but **clarity**.

And for the first time in months, she felt her power come back.
Slow. Steady. Righteous.

> "I'm the one who brings peace. I'm the one who loves hard. I'm the one he should've been chasing."

Not them.

Rule #3: Walk Away Smooth (W.A.S.)
The old Celeste would've shown up to Rico's block, kicked in the door, demanded answers, made noise.

But the new Celeste?

She chose silence.

Because real queens don't argue with Clowns, The Court Jesters.

Three days later, Rico knocked on her door — like he always did when he needed something.

Same cologne. Same grin. Same lies ready to roll.

> "Damn, baby, you been ghosting me. You mad I been grinding? You know I got love for you."

She opened the door, calm as ever. Didn't even flinch.

> "Your stuff's in a box. On the floor. That's all that's left."

He blinked. "Wait… what?"

She stepped aside just enough to let him see the box. Nothing else.

> "I heard you, Rico. In the alley. You and Shayla."

His whole face changed — like someone turned the lights on in a room full of roaches.

He stammered. "That wasn't what it sounded like—"

> "You can keep the excuses," she said. "Matter fact, take them with you."

He looked confused. Angry. Defensive.

> "You really letting go like that? Just like that?"

She met his eyes — steady, unbothered.

> "No screaming. No crying. No show. Just reality. That's how this ends."

He stood there, mouth half-open, trying to find the right move. But the game was over.

He just hadn't realized she flipped the board.

She handed him the box, closed the door behind him, and locked it. Not out of fear.

Out of peace.

No Instagram stories. No cryptic quotes. No warnings.

Just distance.

Because **walking away smooth** doesn't mean walking away soft. It means walking away with nothing left to prove.

The Puppeteer

Shayla sat in the backroom of a dive bar off of East Lennox, legs crossed like a queen on a broken throne. The air was thick with smoke, bass from the main floor pulsing through the walls like a distant heartbeat. She clinked her glass of Henny with her girls, **Nia** and **Keisha**, laughing like the world owed them something.

> "Rico still think he's got it all figured out," Shayla smirked, exhaling a cloud of smoke. "He don't even know he's just another delivery boy. The real plan? We cut him after the next drop. Clean and quiet."

Nia raised a brow as she sipped her drink.

> "And what about Celeste?"

That name hung in the air.

Keisha leaned back, already grinning. She knew the name too.
They all did.
Celeste wasn't just some random girl.
She was the one who used to let Shayla sleep on her couch when rent came up short.
The one who shared her last $20 so Keisha's little boy could eat that weekend.
The one who braided Nia's hair for free the night before her court date, praying over her when no one else would.
They knew her.
And still — they didn't flinch.
Shayla rolled her eyes, like the name was an inconvenience.

"Collateral damage. She'll cry, get over it, and he'll be on to the next. It's not personal."

Keisha snorted.

"That's cold."

Shayla tilted her chin, taking another slow drag from her cigarette.

"Nah. That's survival. The game don't care who gets played. Weak ones get moved like pawns."

She flicked ash into an empty glass and grinned.

"And Celeste? She's the kind that loves loud, trusts easy, and thinks loyalty means everybody got the same heart as her. She ain't built for this."

They all laughed.
Loud. Careless.
What Shayla didn't know —
was that Celeste had already left the game.
She'd heard it all. Felt it all. Let it sting deep enough to wake the part of her that don't cry no more.
This time, she wasn't staying silent.
She wasn't playing nice.
And she damn sure wasn't gonna be someone else's pawn.
They thought they were puppeteers, pulling strings from the dark.

But they forgot one thing —
you can't control a woman who finally remembers her power.

The Bigger Truth

Rico and Shayla thought they were winning.
But they were just rats chasing cheese in a trap they built together.
  Always plotting. Always moving. Never resting.
  Because people who live by manipulation are **never at peace**.
They keep spinning webs until they're tangled in their own.
  Celeste?
  She moved in silence now.
  Focused on her glow. Her growth. Her healing.
  No revenge. No gossip.
Just power.
  She stopped waiting. She knew her damn value.
  And she walked away smooth — like a queen exiting a castle she outgrew.

Same Game, Different Player

You just heard her story — the woman who woke up, wiped her tears, and walked out that door like she never looked back. That's one side of the pain. The side we see more often. The one where the girl gets played, gets wise, and gets gone.
But don't get it twisted.
Men feel too.
Not all of them are players. Not all of them ghost and gaslight. Some of them show up with solid love — only to get spun, lied to, or used as emotional backup plans.

So now we flip it.

Same kind of betrayal.
Same kind of heartbreak.
But this time? It's from the eyes of a man who gave his best —
and had to watch someone treat it like a placeholder.

Because healing ain't just for women.
This is Mason's story.
And this one…
Is for every man who loved real — and had to rise solo.

Played Low, Rose Solo

Mason had a solid heart. He didn't beg for love.

He just showed up real. Ten toes down. Loyal. Steady. Quiet strength. He was the kind of man who showed up when he said he would. He was the kind of man who didn't simply hear your words. He absorbed the silent stories in your eyes and understood the hidden reasons for your smiles, because he always listened with his heart.

He wasn't flashy, but he moved with purpose. Didn't post his heart on timelines — he protected it like sacred ground.

He'd come from environments where trust was earned, not given. Where "I love you" was often a lie told to get something. He didn't come from softness — he came from survival. And somehow, that made his gentleness all the more rare.

So when he gave his heart, it wasn't casual. It was earned. And Jasmine…?

She ain't treat it like that.

Her name was **Jasmine**.

She walked like she knew the world owed her something. Beauty that turned heads and pride that turned stomachs.

Her aura was velvet over razorblades. She had this way of smiling like she was letting you in, while already planning her escape.

Mason wasn't naive. He knew how games got played in the streets. But there was something about Jasmine's brokenness that made him think maybe she just needed something real.

> "She got walls," he told himself.
> "But I got the patience to build a door."

That was the lie that kept him hooked.

He thought he was saving her — but the truth was, she *liked* the chaos. It gave her power. Confusion was her currency.

At first, it was magic. Late-night drives. Smoke sessions under the stars. Deep talks that felt like soul bonding — until he realized she used vulnerability as bait.

She'd cry in his arms and then ghost him the next day. She'd say "I love you" and then dip off the grid till Monday.

> "You know how life be, Mase," she'd shrug. "I'm just grinding. You gotta trust the process."

And he did… until the truth came crashing through like a bullet through stained glass.

Rule #1: Stop Waiting

It started with the little delays.

Waiting for her to text back.

Waiting outside her apartment while she "just touched up her makeup" for 90 minutes.

Waiting for her to explain where she'd been till 3 a.m. — only to hear, "I fell asleep at my cousin's."

Mason cooked dinner one night — shrimp scampi, candles low, playlist vibing. He'd cleaned the place spotless, even wore that cologne she liked.

She hit him with:

> "Ugh babe, something came up. Can we rain check?"

Didn't even call. Just a cold text. Again.

He sat at that table by himself, plate untouched, candles flickering like they were mourning something.

That's when his boy **Jalen** pulled up later.

Walked in, looked around.

> "Yo… You really went all out again, huh?"
>
> Mason gave a tired nod, rubbed the back of his neck.
>
> Jalen leaned back, arms folded.
>
> "Why you treating this chick like royalty when she treating you like a convenience store? Quick stop, no investment."

"She just busy, bro. She grinding—"

> "Nah, Mase. You holding on to a dream version of her, not who she really is. She don't love you — she love the mirror you hold up for her."

That one cut deep.

But Mason still wasn't ready to let go.

He kept waiting.

For her to change.

For her to show up.

For the fantasy to come Tru.

And that's how it happens.

You wait long enough, you start shrinking yourself just to keep the illusion alive.

Mason's heart kept showing up even when her spirit didn't. And every time she flaked, he'd find a reason to stay.

"She been hurt before."
"She just needs to see that I'm not like the rest."
"Maybe next time, she'll get it."

His homie **Jalen, again he** wasn't having it.

"Yo, my guy. Why you keep giving wifey effort to a chick that's barely giving you loyalty crumbs?"
"She different when we're alone, bro."
"Nah," Jalen leaned in. "You're in love with her *potential*. Not her reality."

And that's when Mason had to face it —

He wasn't loving *her*.

He was loving the *idea* of who she could be.

He waited so long for her to change that he forgot to honor who *he* was.

Rule #2: Know Your Worth

It was a Thursday. Mason had just finished a long studio session with one of his new artists. He was tired, hoodie up, keys in hand, walking out of his office tucked behind a black-owned barbershop off Crenshaw.

He shared the lot with a few local businesses — a soul food joint, a vintage sneaker store, and a hookah lounge. They all chipped in for security cams after a few break-ins last year.

As Mason locked the studio door and turned to head out, **Marcus**, the sneaker store owner, called out from his side door.

"Yo Mase! You was up here last night?"

"Nah," Mason replied. "Why, what's up?"

"Some folks was in the lot after hours. I caught it on cam. Thought it might be your people."

Marcus waved him over to the back room and pulled up the footage on a dusty old monitor. The timestamp read *Wednesday — 12:47 a.m.*

There she was.

Jasmine.

In full HD.

Laughing, leaning against the hood of a black Charger with a man Mason didn't recognize — tall, gold teeth, designer hoodie, hand on her waist like it belonged there.

Jasmine was wearing the same jacket Mason had bought her. The same one she claimed she "left at her cousin's."

Mason stood still, jaw clenched, heart cold.

Then came the audio — slightly fuzzy, but clear enough to sting.

> "Mason?" Jasmine giggled. "Please. He's sweet. But he's just my peacekeeper. My fallback. I tell him I'm tired, and he sends food and flowers. That's what he's good for."

The man laughed.

> "So he don't know?"
>
> "Nah. He still think he the King," Jasmine smirked. "But I'm out here moving like a queen. Multiple thrones, baby."

Mason didn't flinch.

Didn't curse.

Didn't even speak.

He just watched.

Frame by frame.

That's when he realized…

She never respected him.

She just liked the comfort he gave her.

She used his peace as her playground.

Back at his apartment, he sat in silence.

No music. No distractions. Just a cold drink in one hand and the remote in the other — volume muted, screen dark.

He thought about the ride shares she charged to his account.

The nights she slept over, only to dip before sunrise.

The "dead phone battery" lies.

The times he poured love into a woman who used his presence to patch her emptiness.

And that's when it hit:

> "She ain't outsmart me…
> I betrayed myself — by trusting a woman I *knew* wasn't built for what I gave."

He didn't break. He **clarified**. And in that stillness, **Rule #2** was born.
Know your worth, bro. Or somebody else will price you cheap.

Rule #3: Walk Away Smooth (W.A.S.)

The old Mason?

He would've lost it.

Pulled up to her spot hot, voice raised, looking for explanations she would've danced around with lies. He would've played into her drama like a scene from a cheap soap opera.

But the man who sat in that dim room, watching Jasmine's betrayal on a flickering monitor?

That Mason…

Moved different.

He didn't send her the footage.

Didn't text her.

Didn't even let his anger write a post for social media.

He just **unplugged**.

Three days later, she called.

> **Jasmine**: "Hey stranger… you been ghosting me. What's up with that? You mad I've been busy or something?"

Her voice was all sugar and nerve.

Mason's tone was steel wrapped in calm.

> **Mason**: "Your stuff's in the trunk. I'll be at your building in ten. I ain't coming up."

There was a pause.

Then laughter.

"Mason… are you serious right now? You really doing all this over some vibe shift?"

"Nah," he replied, unlocking his door, stepping into the elevator of her building. "This ain't about vibes. It's about value. Mine."

Ten minutes later, Jasmine strutted out of her apartment in a silk robe, eyebrows on fleek, acting like she was starring in a breakup music video.

"You breaking up with me or something?" she smirked, walking up to the car.

"Nah," Mason said, popping the trunk. "I'm just done pretending you were ever really with me."

Her smirk twitched.

"Come on, you acting dramatic. I don't know what you think you saw or heard—"

"I didn't think," he cut her off, eyes locked. "I watched you. In 1080p. You and gold-teeth buddy, laughing like my name was a joke."

Jasmine's face fell.

He didn't wait for the scramble.

Didn't give her a monologue.

Didn't give her a chance to cry and fake vulnerability again.

"And don't worry," he added, walking back to his car.
"I'm not mad."
"Then why—?"
"Because I don't beg for people to choose me.
 I give them the space to walk out.
 And the clarity to never let them back in."

He got in, turned the key, and pulled off.
 Smooth. No skid. No glance back.
 He didn't need closure.
 He gave himself peace.
 Because once you know your worth?
 You don't wait.
 You don't chase.
 You **exit like royalty.**

In The Shadow

Downtown. Late night. Red lights reflecting off wine glasses. A lounge with low ceilings, moody music, and quiet secrets.

Jasmine sat in a curved velvet booth with **Tiana** and **Zoey**. Lip gloss perfect, nails sharp, but her energy was off. She'd been staring at her phone for the past hour, refreshing, checking, waiting.

Still no texts.

Still no "hey, you up?"

Still no Mason.

Tiana sipped her drink slow, watching her.

"So… you really think he's coming back?"

Jasmine scoffed.

"Girl, please. Mason always circles back. He just emotional right now. Probably somewhere journaling and burning sage."

Zoey raised an eyebrow.

"You sure? 'Cause the way he dropped your stuff off like it was a business transaction… that didn't look like a 'come back later' move."

"He tripping' over some footage," Jasmine waved her hand like it meant nothing. "He saw some old-ass security camera clip. Me and Dre was just talking. That angle made it look wild."

Tiana frowned.

"Old clip? Jas… that was from, like, two nights ago."
"Whatever. It's not like I was kissing dude on camera."

Zoey leaned in, voice low.

"But you *was* talking reckless. He told me he heard the audio. You said he was your fallback."

"I ain't say it like *that*," Jasmine snapped. Then caught herself. Smoothed her tone. "Y'all know how I be playing sometimes. He wasn't even supposed to hear that part."

Tiana folded her arms, her voice cooler than usual.

"You ain't just play him, Jas. You played yourself."

Jasmine tried to laugh it off, but her throat was dry.

"Y'all acting like I committed a crime. Mason's grown. He'll get over it."

"You didn't just hurt a dude," Tiana said, looking her dead in the eye. "You hurt a *good* one. He did everything for you, and you used him like a backup charger."

Jasmine looked away, suddenly fascinated by the bottom of her wine glass.

"He ain't perfect either," she muttered.

Zoey gave her a look.

"Yeah, but he was *present*. He showed up. You didn't."

Tiana leaned back, letting the silence hit.

> "You thought he was too soft to walk.
> But real ones don't chase forever.
> Eventually, they choose peace over potential."

Jasmine stared at her phone one more time.
Still no message.
No missed calls.
No passive-aggressive meme posts.
Nothing.
Just **silence**.

"He'll hit me," she mumbled. "He always does."

But even as she said it, her voice cracked like she didn't believe it anymore.
Zoey sighed, shaking her head.

> "Nah, Jas.
> He saw it all.
> He heard it all.
> And this time?
> He finally chose *himself*."

And somewhere across town, in a quiet apartment lit by focus and not regret, Mason was pouring a drink for himself, not her. Focused. Free.

Because **when a good man finally sees the game for what it is… he don't play it again.**

The Bigger Truth

Jasmine thought she won.

Thought silence meant confusion.

That no reaction meant weakness.

But Mason wasn't silent.

He was **processing.**

And now?

He wasn't hurt.

He was **healed**.

He deleted her number — not out of rage, but to make room for peace.

He upgraded his circle — friends who challenged him, not just clapped for him.

He re-invested in himself — not to glow up for revenge, but to realign with his mission.

He poured the love he once gave her into his business, his fitness, and his foundation for at-risk youth.

No subposts.

No "look at me now" stories.

No bitterness.

Just **elevation**.

Because when a man learns his worth, everything around him changes.

>The calls slow down.
>The circles shrink.
>The distractions fall off.
>And what's left… is **power**.

He didn't need her to apologize.
    He didn't need closure.
    He didn't need revenge.
    He just needed the truth.
    And he got it on camera.

When Real Recognizes Real

Six months later.

It's spring. Sunlight golden over the concrete. Birds flying between the streetlamps. Mason's world? Clearer than it's ever been.

He's at an open mic night he sponsored for local creatives — fresh talent, clean energy. No egos. No games. Just authenticity.

He wasn't looking for love.

And that's usually when it finds you.

Her name was **Zaria**.

She walked in wearing no mask, no performance. Just truth in human form. Natural hair, brown eyes deep like they carried soul archives.

She performed last.

No glitter. No flair. Just her and the mic.

> "This poem," she said, "is about when a man finally learns he don't have to bleed to prove he's loving right."

She looked out, and her eyes found **him**.

Mason felt it in his chest. That familiar ache. But this time, it wasn't pain. It was… recognition.

After the show, she approached him. No flirting. No small talk. Just energy.

> "You the man behind the mic night?"
> "Yeah," he nodded. "You the one who left the room breathless."

Zaria smiled, slow and real.

"I saw you during my set. You didn't just hear me — you *heard* me."

"I try not to miss the real ones anymore."

She tilted her head.

"Been through something?"

"Yeah. But I healed through it. Solo."

She nodded. No judgment. No rush.

"Well… if peace ever needs company," she said softly, "I'm around."

The Final Truth

Mason didn't fall in love that night.

He didn't need to.

He'd already fallen **in line with himself.**

Zaria didn't fix him. She just saw the version he fought hard to become — and met him there.

No more waiting.

No more chasing.

No more trying to be enough for people who saw him as convenient.

He wasn't played low anymore.

He had risen solo.

And this time?

He stayed there.

SECTION 2

THE QUEEN'S CODE

To the Queens: This is your mirror.
To the Kings: This is your map.

Let me make something real clear before we dive in—
I didn't write this part just for women.

I wrote it for men as well.
I wrote it **like I was advising my own daughter**.
Not just to protect her from this cold world, but to **prepare her** to walk through it crowned, calm, and untouchable.
I wrote it for every woman who's ever questioned her worth, dropped her standards, or forgot how divine she is—just to feel chosen by someone who ain't even qualified to sit beside her.

This is a manual for Queens who are done shrinking.
It's for the ones tired of chasing love and ready to start **commanding respect**.

But if you're man reading this?
Don't skip a single word.

Because *this right here* is your **blueprint**, too.
This section shows you what real Royalty looks like in a woman—
So you stop mistaking curves for character.
So you stop giving the throne to a stranger who don't know how to build, hold, or respect a kingdom.

When you know the code of a Queen,
You stop entertaining energy that only drains you.
You stop falling for pretty chaos and start standing beside **power wrapped in peace**.

So Queens—
Read this like it's armor.
Like it's a love letter from someone who sees your value even when the world refuses to.
Let it check you. Let it crown you. Let it raise your standards.

And Kings—
Study this like a playbook.
This ain't about control, this is about **compatibility**.
About choosing women who bring legacy, not lessons you didn't ask for.

Because when a real King meets a real Queen,
They don't put each other down.

They help each other with their Crowns.
They compete with each other, so they complete with each other.

We just tossed that dead weight to the curb – and best believe, that sh*t better be gone for good. The lessons from that last section? They're etched in concrete now, a blueprint for the sovereign you're becoming. You learned to stop waiting on ghosts, to recognize your own damn value, and to Walk Away Smooth. That ain't just theory, that's survival code for these streets.

It's time to peel back the layers and truly peep who the genuine Queens are in this twisted game. See, out in these streets, a lot of folks are walking around sideways, straight-up clueless, getting played by the very individuals they're trying to win over. But peep this: you're holding the damn cheat code right here in your hands. This is the raw truth, the unfiltered wisdom that you need to navigate this game like the Royalty you are.

Alright, check it. We ain't gon' sugarcoat nothing. This ain't no pep rally; this is straight-up game you need to survive and thrive in these streets. See, I'm dropping this wisdom like I'm speaking directly to a future generation. 'Cause the principles? They don't change. **Respect, power, knowing your worth** – that's universal. It applies whether you're building your empire or recognizing a Tru Queen for the throne.

So check it, Royals in the making. You gotta understand, this ain't about playing small or begging for scraps. This is about recognizing the fire you got inside and letting that blaze. Every person born is a Royalty. Don't let nobody dim your shine. Learn the rules, then break the ones that hold you back. Stand tall, move with intention, and let the world know you ain't to be played with. This ain't a request; it's a Got-Damn decree. Get it? Got it? Good. Now let's get to it. This is *The Queen's Code*.

Read it slow.
Absorb it deep.
And never again confuse attention with value.

"QUEEN'S CODE"

Listen up, shawty, your dad want you prepared,
I'm the realest to tell you, that "life ain't fair."

You my Princess forever, but be a Queen one day,
I'm not gon' be here always, so check what I gotta say.

One day there will be a real man or a joke.
So don't ever lose my voice, baby, and here's the code.

She don't bow, she don't break, she don't play no fool,
She got grace in her stride, but her heart stay cool.

She don't chase no clout, she just walk with flame,
Ain't no shame in her tone when she speak his name.

Rule one—show respect, but don't hand it for free,
He a king when he earned it, not 'cause he says he be.

Her intellect, the scale, ain't no need for drama,
If his backbone prevail, she moves like karma.

Rule two—stay modest, got class on lock,
She don't need short skirts to make 'em jaws drop.

No filters, no fronting, ain't no thirst in her frame,
Just raw truth in the lens, can't nobody claim.

She the prize that they chase, the whisper in the night,
But her soul ain't for rent, outta every man's sight

Forget the IG bait, the angles and the pose,
Her real- life frame's flawless, everybody knows.

And every Brotha wants her, try to run that game,
But she built too different, can't nobody tame.

Eyes on her King, she don't trip off the rest,
When other dudes try, she dismiss'em with finesse.

Says, "I'm taken, baby, step back with grace,"
Loyalty loud in her silence and face.

Rule three—compassion, she soft but she's real,
She's his peace, not his pain, she the balm, not the steel.

She don't bark when he's down, she just sit and vibe,
Whispers, "You got this baby" while he tries to rise.

She don't bash him, holds the ground when it's deep,
Knows when to dash, but this Queen runs steep.

Not a pushover, but she tender, divine,
She's the calm in the storm, when he's walking that line.

Rule four—keep him close, with that confident glow,
She ain't begging for love, 'cause Queens don't stoop low.

She's the type you remember, the vibe you don't fake,
Every move she make got that high-stakes grace.

Got love in her hands, but her soul don't fold,
She the rarest of gems, she the Queen made of gold.

So salute to the women who walk with that code,
Crown on straight, no heavy episode.

They don't flex loud—they move like waves,
Queens in the jungle, beauty and brave.

Rule #1: Respect the Real (The Royal Decree)

SUNNY MASTERPEACE

My young Queen, my baby girl, peep this. The very essence of the Queen's Code, the first truth etched in your spirit, the bedrock your empire will rise upon, is this: **respect ain't no weakness you're flashing, no soft spot for the vultures to peck at.** Nah, respect is that razor-sharp intuition, that sixth sense that hums in your bones, telling you who's genuine and who's just a damn mirage in the desert. It's the street smarts you live by when you out here navigating the concrete labyrinth, discerning the authentic from the fake. It's about knowing in your soul who deserves even a flicker of your precious light and who deserves the absolute zero, the cold shoulder that freezes their weak intentions dead in their tracks. Feel me? This ain't about being nice; it's about being *discerning*.

Think of it like this, baby girl, the way you carry yourself, the energy you project, the very air that moves around you? **That's your crown before you even utter a single damn word.** It ain't about bending a knee to nobody, no matter how shiny their facade. It ain't about playing the damsel in distress, waiting for some hero to swoop in and validate your existence. Hell nah. It's about having that eagle eye, that internal radar to spot the Tru strength, the unwavering character, not just in yourself, but in others. It's about that deep, unshakable inner control, that quiet power that resonates louder than any shouting, that speaks volumes without a single syllable. And peep the real leaders out here, the ones who leave a legacy, not just a fleeting impression. They're the ones whose very presence inspires you to dig deeper, to push harder, to excavate that inherent Royalty that's already blazing within you, waiting to be unleashed.

Now, a Tru Queen on her throne? She ain't just throwing around respect like it's confetti at a parade. She ain't handing out participation trophies for simply showing up. **That joint? They gotta earn it.** They gotta demonstrate it. It ain't a given because some smooth-talking cat with a slick line thinks he's entitled to your attention, your time, or your reverence. Uh-uh. A Queen is always observing, always analyzing his every damn move, his consistency, his character when the lights are off. She might even throw a little curve-ball his way, not to be a straight-up villain playing games, but to test the very foundation of his being. Is he built on solid ground, forged in real fire, or is he just a house of cards ready to crumble at the first breath of adversity? When a man can stand his own, when he can hold his head high without losing himself in the drama, without bending to manipulation or dissolving into weakness? Boom. That's when she bestows that genuine, hard-earned respect. And that respect, that's the rich, fertile soil where something truly real can take root – that deep, unspoken trust, that unbreakable bond of intimacy that transcends the superficial. It's the absolute foundation of any empire worth building, feel me?

And check this out, my warrior Princess, this respect thing ain't just a one-way street, a payment you dispense. When you give it genuinely to those who earn it, it's a powerful force that elevates the entire damn relationship. It's a silent affirmation, a recognition that lets a real man know that you truly see him, that you appreciate the raw, powerful masculine energy he brings to the table – that inherent provider instinct, that unwavering protector vibe. But listen close, this ain't about you diminishing yourself, playing small, or shrinking your light to make him feel bigger. Hell nah. It's about both of y'all rising together, each a force in your own right, reaching for higher ground, building something monumental that can withstand any storm.

Respect? It's like building walls, but the good kind. It constructs an invisible but impenetrable boundary, a clear declaration that lets folks know exactly where they stand in your kingdom. Treat folks like they matter, and watch how they ride for you. That's a Tru Queen energy. You ain't gotta be screaming and throwing tantrums like a child to show your power, to make your point. Nah, Tru power whispers. It resonates. **Respect teaches you to speak with that quiet, regal dignity, that Queenly authority** that commands attention not through volume or aggression, but through the sheer weight of your presence. Be classy, show love, get love. That's the crown you earn, not the one they give you. An with that crown, you will own every damn space you walk into, commanding attention with your very being. Plant respect, harvest loyalty. That's the street smarts of a Tru Queen.

The Unseen Armor of Discerning Reverence

Let's unpack this further, lil mama. Your respect is a shield, not a weapon. It protects your spirit from the poison of those who seek to drain you. How you choose to bestow it, or withhold it, shapes your reality. A Queen doesn't give her respect to just anyone; she *discerns*. She has a built-in bullsh*t detector that hums when something ain't right. This ain't about being judgmental, it's about being **wise**. It's about valuing your peace over pandering to popularity.

You know the types out there – the smooth talkers who've mastered the art of illusion, the manipulators who whisper sweet nothing while their actions scream disrespect. Your respect is too valuable to be wasted on such charades. You must learn to read beyond the words, to feel the intent behind the gestures. Does their respect feel genuine, or does it feel like a calculated play? Does it uplift you, or does it feel conditional, designed to keep you in check? A Queen recognizes that Tru respect flows from a place of integrity, not from a desire to control or diminish. And when you withhold your respect from those who haven't earned it, you're not being cruel; you're honoring your own inherent divinity.

The Magnet for Real Leadership (Expanded)

And this is crucial, baby girl. Respect? It's a damn magnet for real leadership. It draws in the Kings, the architects, the visionaries. The right people into your circle. So, check it. Them insecure cats, the weak ones who couldn't lead a parade down a straight street, they be running their mouths like they own the whole block, trying to be the only voice you hear, the only source of "truth" in your world. They're feeding you scraps of information, keeping you deliberately in the dark, scared you gonna stumble upon a real King with some genuine wisdom, someone who'll drop truth bombs that shatter their fragile illusions and open your eyes to a whole different world, a different level of existence. They be sweating bullets, baby girl, thinking you gonna wise up, see through their weak game, and roll with a crew that's actually going somewhere, building something real, not just talking about it. They see that knowledge dropping like a beat that's gonna make you move to a different rhythm, a rhythm they can't control, a dance they can't lead.

But a real leader? He ain't gotta shout to be heard. His presence, his actions, his genuine knowledge speaks for itself. He ain't threatened if you listen to other voices, if you seek knowledge from other sources; he knows truth stands on its own, undeniable and powerful. He's confident that genuine insight will always resonate with a mind like yours, a Queen's mind. He welcomes you learning and growing, 'cause he understands that a strong mind, an empowered partner, makes for a stronger movement, a more formidable empire. He ain't trying to hold you back; he's actively trying to elevate the whole damn game, to push you to your highest potential.

A Queen? You gotta have the street smarts, the inner wisdom, to discern the profound difference between these two types of men. One wants to control your light; the other wants to amplify it. One fears your growth; the other champions it. And only that strong, grounded man, the one who leads with his mind and his heart in sync, the one who embodies Tru respect in his every action, only he earns your unbreakable loyalty, your fierce, unyielding devotion.

A woman who throws shade and disrespect like it's going out of style, who thrives on drama and belittles others? She might get some fleeting attention, some rubberneckers looking at the spectacle, like a car crash on the freeway. But she ain't gonna hold onto a good man's soul, not the kind of man a Queen truly desires. That connection won't be real; it'll be built on sand, crumbling at the first real storm. But you, my Princess, if you carry yourself with that Queenly respect, if you demand it without even saying a word, if your presence alone dictates the level of reverence you receive? Man, **you leave a permanent mark. You become unforgettable, a legend whispered in the halls of power. You become absolutely irreplaceable in his world, a cornerstone, not a temporary fixture.** That's the power you wield, the crown you wear. Remember that, always.

The Irreplaceable Status (Expanded)

Alright, you feeling that, deep in your gut? But we ain't even close to being done yet. Let's dig even deeper, peel back another layer of this Queenly code on respect, revealing the Tru treasure beneath.

And peep this, shawty. That irreplaceable status? It ain't just about how he sees you. It's about **the sacred, unshakable space you cultivate within yourself**. When you move with this A-to-Z Respect, you cultivate a certain kind of inner peace, a rock-solid self-assuredness that radiates outward like the sun. You ain't chasing validation from external sources, because you already *know* your worth down to your damn bones. You ain't gotta get messy, you ain't gotta stoop to petty drama, because you carry yourself with a quiet storm inside, a calm authority that commands attention without effort. That respect you demand from others? It begins and ends with the absolute, non-negotiable respect you have for yourself. You gotta value your mind, that sharp intellect; your body, that sacred temple; your spirit, that divine fire within you. You gotta know your boundaries, those invisible lines that protect your peace, and you gotta stand firm on 'em like an ancient oak, unmoving in the face of any wind.

Think about it, really feel this. A Queen in her kingdom? She ain't worried about every little peasant throwing shade, every whisper of jealousy from the shadows. She moves with an undeniable purpose, with inherent grace, knowing her position, her power, her divine right. When you operate from a place of **unyielding self-respect – for yourself first, and then for those rare few who truly earn it** – you don't just attract; you *create* a different kind of atmosphere around you. You don't just attract quality; you *demand* it through your very being. You automatically filter out the noise, the negativity, the low-vibration energy. Them petty games, them childish squabbles, them manipulative tactics? They just bounce right off you like bullets off Vibranium, 'cause you operating on a higher frequency, a different plane of existence. And this ain't about being perfect, lil mama, feel? Nobody's perfect. Everybody stumbles, everybody makes mistakes, takes an L. But a Tru Queen? She owns that. She doesn't deny her flaws; she learns from them, extracts the wisdom like gold from rock. And she keeps it moving with respect and with her dignity intact, unmarred by past missteps. She don't try to justify it, but she don't let nobody else define her worth through her mistakes either.

So when you step out there, baby girl, remember this truth, let it resonate in every cell. And that respect you carry? **It's your shield and your sword, forged in the fires of self-knowledge.** It protects your spirit from the venom of disrespect, and it commands attention in the right way, from the right people. **Your Circle Reflects**

Your Crown, feel me? The company you keep? That's a direct reflection of the respect you have for yourself. A Queen doesn't surround herself with jesters, with gossips, or with those who secretly wish for her downfall. Nah. Your circle is your sanctuary, your battleground, and your source of fuel. **Respect means choosing those who elevate you, who challenge you to be better, who celebrate your wins and lift you when you stumble, and to listen. I mean real listening. Something you learn quick on the block. See, every act of respect, no matter how small, its like a hand reaching out, pulling someone a little higher. It says, "I see you. I acknowledge your hustle, and your sacrifices, and Your life matters." And when you feel seen, when you feel that genuine nod of understanding? That can lift you up when you're on your knees. It remind you of your own worth, the fire you got inside. And that fire? It will forge the crown on your head. The best crown to wear.**

If you got folks in your corner who ain't respecting your grind, who ain't respecting your boundaries, who are constantly bringing drama to your doorstep? That's a red flag waving in your face, baby girl. And respecting yourself means having the courage to prune those branches, to sever those ties, even if it hurts for a minute. Because when you tolerate disrespect in your inner circle, you're subtly telling the world, and yourself, that it's okay. And it ain't. A Tru Queen knows her worth too much to let her crown be tarnished by low-vibration company. Your peace is paramount, and your inner circle should reflect the high value you place on it. That will show the world that you ain't no pushover, no easy target, but you also ain't gotta be ruthless or aggressive to be real. You're a force to be reckoned with, not through brute aggression, but through the quiet, unshakable power of your self-respect and the discerning, intentional way you give it to others, and having that tight circle of people who you truly respect and trust. That's the undeniable mark of a Tru Queen. That's how you leave a legacy that ain't just about being remembered, but about being revered, cherished, and looked up to. You dig? Keep that fire in your heart, that wisdom in your mind, and that respect in your stride. But you can't get to that place without Knowing yourself, so then you can respect and honor yourself. That's your Royal decree.

Rule #2: Be Modest

Alright, let's break down this "Be Modest" joint, Queen style. This ain't about playing invisible; it's about knowing your worth without having to scream it from the rooftops.

Peep this, baby girl, **modesty ain't about hiding in the shadows.** It's about knowing you're that damn prize, so you ain't gotta be shaking your assets for every Tom, Dick, and Harry. In this rigged game they playing, they try to sell modesty like it's a worn-out cloak, something to hide your shine. They want you begging for applause, chasing every fleeting spotlight. But a Tru Queen? She moves with a different kind of glow. What you got right here, baby girl? This ain't just words; it's a map to your own damn throne.

"Modesty ain't weakness; it's a vault holding something priceless." Think about that. You got something inside you that's straight fire, something they can't touch or take. Modesty? That's the steel door on that vault. It ain't about hiding your worth; it's about protecting the real gems.

"It's a silent force that commands attention without a single shout." You ever walk into a room and just feel somebody's presence? They ain't gotta be the loudest one; they just got that energy. That's the power of quiet confidence. It hits different.

"It's that deep breath before the storm hits – quiet power gathering strength." Life gonna throw punches, no doubt. But that moment you take to breathe, to center yourself? That's you tapping into that quiet power. It's the calm before you unleash your greatness.

"It's that unwavering gaze that speaks volumes while others are just making noises." People love to yap, to brag, to fill the air with nothing. But your eyes? They can tell a whole story without saying a damn word. That focus, that knowing look? That's real.

"It's that truth dropped in a hushed room that echoes louder than any empty boast in a stadium." When you speak your truth, even if it's quiet, it carries weight. It cuts through the BS. Those loud mouths? They fade. Your truth? It shines to conquer any darkness of doubt.

It's the kind of power that doesn't need validation; it radiates from a core of pure knowing. You don't need nobody to tell you who you are. You know. That inner knowing? That's your superpower. It's the quiet confidence that inspires folks to listen closer, 'cause they sense something real and unbreakable. People are hungry for what's real. When you move with that quiet confidence, they lean in. They know you ain't playing games. Feel?

They out here thinking modesty is about dimming your own light, playing small so nobody feels insecure. Let me remind you baby girl, That's their small thinking. Don't ever shrink yourself for nobody. But a real Queen? She knows her shine is undeniable, so she ain't gotta blind nobody with it. You gonna shine, my Princess. It's in your DNA. But you ain't gotta be all up in people's faces about it.

The Tru Queen? Her power speaks for itself, like a diamond that don't need a spotlight to sparkle. You are that diamond. You got that inner brilliance. You don't need the flashing lights to prove your worth. Your actions, your character? That's the sparkle they can't ignore.

So yeah, feel that. Let it sink in. This ain't just about being quiet; it's about being solid. It's about knowing your worth without screaming it from the rooftops. It's about having that inner fire that burns steady and bright. The louder you are, the weaker you are. Most of the time, it's the one sitting quiet, observing, knowing exactly what she brings to the table without needing to announce it. Not 'cause she's shy or can't think of any words to say, it's 'cause she don't waste her time, energy, and words on nonsense, fruitless arguments. Her words are heavy and strong 'cause her confidence is the silence that makes everyone else hush up and listen when she finally speaks. It's the unspoken strength that commands respect, 'cause they know real value doesn't need a sales pitch. That's the Tru power of a Queen's modesty.

Quality Over Quantity: The Royal Standard

This ain't about chasing every spotlight, nah. She ain't out here fronting for the Gram or trying to be the center of every damn circle. That's small time, a quick hit, and then it's gone. She's on a whole 'nother vibe. She's looking for that one, that real one, the one who cuts through all the noise and truly sees her. Not just the surface, not just the packaging, but the raw, uncut truth of who she is inside. When that gaze connects, when that soul-to-soul recognition happens? That's the ultimate come-up. That's the real win.

See, her beauty ain't no cheap knock-off, no costume jewelry glinting in the sun. Nah, **it's that pure gold, refined and rare, shining with a quiet fire.** It ain't screaming for attention 'cause it don't gotta. And her confidence? Forget that loud, chest-thumping energy. Hers is deep, steady like a heartbeat in the trenches, calm and real. It's the confidence of someone who knows her own worth, not because someone told her, but because she built it, brick by brick, from the ground up.

She ain't out here begging for no handouts of attention. Her value ain't determined by how many likes she gets or how many heads she turns. Nah, **her worth is in the eyes of the one who truly sees her**, who understands the depths of her grind, the layers of her soul.

Think about it like this: you got your fast-food joints, open to everybody, quick and easy. But then you got that exclusive spot, the one with the reservation, where you gotta dress proper. They ain't just letting anybody in, right? They hold a certain standard, they know their worth. That's her. She's that exclusive experience, not for the masses, but for the one who's truly ready to appreciate the realest. Dig what I'm saying?

Modesty ain't insecurity, feel? It's rock-solid self-assurance. You ain't gotta put everything on display to prove you got it. The real power moves? They happen in silence, in the unspoken understanding, not in the chaos and the noise. Think about them backrooms where the real deals go down – ain't no shouting match there.

When some thirsty dude approaches? She ain't gonna flinch or get all awkward. She gonna turn down that unwanted attention with grace, with that Queenly poise, 'cause she already got the admiration that truly matters, the kind that comes from genuine respect, not fleeting lust. It's not about being stuck up, 'cause there's a difference between valuing what's sacred to her and being rude, all 'cause she's insecure and trying to protect her heart in the wrong way. Her words? They ain't just throwaway lines. Her body? It ain't public property. Her time? That's gold. She understands that what's valuable ain't what's cheap and easy to get. It's the rare gem, the one you gotta earn, the one that ain't just freely available to every wannabes from the Waneebe tribe.

So, in her modesty, she's sending a clear message: she ain't out here trying to impress every scrub that walks by. She's got her eyes set on the one who's worthy, the one who's earned a place in her world. And a woman like that? That's fuego, a rare find. That's the kind of Queen that makes a King step his game up. Remember that, baby girl. Your mystery is your power. Don't give it away for free.

The Law of Scarcity: The Tru Value Of Products

You feeling that quiet power? Now, let it resonate even deeper into your understanding, my young Queen.

And peep this, shawty, that mystery that modesty creates? It ain't about playing games or being deceitful. It's about preserving your essence, keeping something sacred for the right soul to discover. Think of it like a hidden treasure. If it's just lying out in the open, everybody can grab a piece, and its value diminishes. **It's called the law of scarcity.** Scarcity is like when the block's running low on something everyone wants. Everybody wants a piece, right? But there ain't enough to go around.

Think about it: the freshest kicks that just dropped. Mad hype, everyone wants 'em, but the store only got a limited stock. That's scarcity. Not everybody gonna walk away with a pair. So them shoes prices are sky high. It's the same with anything valuable. Whether it's money, respect on the streets, or a loyal crew – there's only so much of it out there. You gotta hustle, make smart choices, 'cause it ain't just gonna fall in your lap. Limited supply, high demand. You feel me? Especially when it comes to dudes, their desire for females is relentless, so if you're just giving sh*t out freely, who's gonna value that? Think about it for a sec, air, water, and food are essential for our survival, right? But why is it that diamonds, gold, and every precious gem are more expensive than air, water, and food, when you can't eat rocks to survive? **It's the law of scarcity, baby!** But when it's guarded, when it's revealed only to those who truly seek it and appreciate its worth? That's when its power truly shines.

This ain't about being afraid to be seen or to own your beauty. Hell nah. It's about having the wisdom to know when and for whom you unveil those layers. It's about understanding that Tru connection ain't built on superficial flash, but on genuine appreciation for who you are, inside and out. Them cats who are just drawn to the obvious? They ain't seeing you. They're seeing a spectacle. But the one who's drawn to your quiet strength, to the depth beneath the surface? That's the one who's truly seeing the Queen in you.

And that self-assurance that comes with modesty? It's like having a vault inside you, filled with your worth. You ain't gotta open it up and show everybody the jewels just to prove they're there. You know they're there. That quiet sun, that bright confidence radiates from within, and the right people will recognize it. They'll be drawn to that inner light, that unspoken power.

Think about the most **powerful** and **honorable** figures in history. They didn't always need to be the loudest in the room. Their presence commanded respect. Their words carried weight because they weren't thrown around carelessly. That's the essence of modest power. It's about knowing your value so deeply that you don't feel the need to constantly seek external validation.

The Silent Flex: Power in the Unspoken

Alright, check it. Modesty ain't just being humble; it's **low-key flexing your inner Boss.** It's like having a Lambo but pulling up in something clean and understated. The heads still turn 'cause they sense the real deal.

It's playing your cards close to the chest, letting your moves speak louder than your mouth ever could. While they're out here shouting about their wins, you're quietly stacking yours, making 'em wonder what you got up your sleeve.

Think of it like this: the most valuable art doesn't need a neon sign. It hangs in a gallery, and those who know, knows. Your worth ain't gotta be advertised; the right eyes will recognize it.

It's about having that quiet storm inside you. You ain't gotta be loud to be powerful. It's about having that patient. Sometimes, the deepest impact comes from the silence, from the knowing glance that says, "I got this," without uttering a single word.

It's like being the smartest person in the room but letting others run their mouths. You listen, you learn, and when you finally speak, it hits different 'cause they know you ain't just talking noise. You are speaking from a place of patient and solution by understanding everyone's noise. Your mind is clear and your words are heavy.

So yeah, modesty? It's the ultimate stealth mode for a G. You move with grace, you operate with wisdom, and your impact? It's undeniable, even when you ain't trying to be the loudest in the crowd. It's a silent flex that screams volumes to those who are really paying attention.

So, as you navigate this world, baby girl, remember the power of holding back, of not revealing everything all at once. Let them peel back the layers, let them earn the privilege of seeing the depths of who you are. Your words, your time, your energy? These are precious commodities. Invest them wisely with those who truly appreciate their value. Don't be afraid to be selective. Don't be afraid to say no. Your sacredness is your strength. And in that modesty, you ain't just preserving yourself. You're revealing that you're not just any woman and that you're a rare gem, a Tru Queen who knows her worth ain't up for grabs. Feel? Let that quiet power be your signature.

THE ANTIDOTE

Rule #3: Master the Code of Compassion

Aight, listen up, baby girl. This ain't just some suggestion you can skim over; this is a **mandate**, a fundamental truth etched into the very fabric of how you command respect and truly, genuinely, lock down a King's heart. This right here? This is the secret sauce, the unspoken language of power, the blueprint for how you elevate beyond just being a "woman" and ascend to Tru Queen status. So, listen up, let every word resonate in your spirit, 'cause this ain't just about a moment; it's about building a dynasty.

Compassion ain't about being a sucka. It's not about being naive, or weak, or letting folks run game on you. Nah. That's a rookie mistake, a street trap. Tru compassion, the kind we're talking about? It's your superpower, your ultimate weapon in a world that often values hardness over heart. It's that undeniable force that can heal a brother down to his very bones, stitch up wounds he didn't even know he had, keep him grounded when the world tries to shake his very foundation, and build something so damn resilient, so damn unbreakable, that it laughs in the face of adversity, generational curses, and all the chaos life throws at it. This is where you don't just survive; this is where you thrive and build a legacy that echoes through time.

Now I ain't talking about that surface-level, Instagram-quote, "I'm here for you" type love. I'm talking 'bout that deep-rooted, unshakable, "I see you when you can't even see yourself" type of compassion. The type that don't flinch when he's at his lowest, when he's tryna figure himself out, when life got him in a choke-hold and he don't even got the words for what he feeling. See, a man, your man, steps out into that unforgiving jungle every single day. He's battling silent wars, fighting his own demons, silencing the internal doubts, navigating treacherous territories, and confronting pressures that would break a lesser spirit. He's out there on the block, in the boardroom, in the streets, on the grind, putting on that tough exterior, that impenetrable armor, just to survive the sheer brutality of it all, to protect the raw vulnerability he keeps hidden deep inside. He's got to be a strategist, a provider, a protector. But imagine this, envision the scene: if he comes home, to you, his supposed haven, his sanctuary, the place he should feel safe, and all he finds is a brick wall, a cold shoulder, more judgment, more demands, or another damn storm raging in his own living room? He's still out there on his own, even within the confines of his own crib. He's isolated, feeling like he's fighting on all fronts – the outside world and his own home – with no safe ground to stand on, no place to truly mend his wounds, no genuine hand to steady him. That ain't a partnership, that's just an extension of the war zone, a constant state of alert that will eventually drain him dry.

A Tru Queen, a woman deeply rooted in her wisdom and genuinely understanding her real power, she recognizes her role ain't to add to the chaos, to be another obstacle in his already challenging life. Her strength, her undeniable influence, lies in being his peace, his sanctuary, the calm in the very eye of his hurricane. She treats her man with that deep, soul-level compassion because she sees past the bravado, past the tough-guy act he puts on for the world to witness. She possesses the insight to know the invisible weight he's carrying on his shoulders, the silent battles he's fighting within himself, the anxieties that gnaw at him, even when he ain't saying a single damn word or explicitly asking for a thing. She truly gets that just 'cause he's built like a warrior, strong and seemingly impervious, don't mean he don't need softness, don't mean he don't need a tender touch, a nurturing spirit, a soft place to land. In fact, the raw, uncut truth is, he probably needs that tenderness, that understanding, that unwavering support, more than he'll ever let on, more than he'll ever admit, even to himself, because society often tells him vulnerability is weakness. See, any woman can be there when a man is winning, when he got money in his pocket, when he's smelling good and moving with confidence. But can you be there when he's broken? When he is questioning his worth? When he feel like the world done forgot about him? That's where your Royalty show.

Compassion ain't weakness, ma. It's power. It's the strength to hold space without judging. It's knowing when to speak and when to just sit in silence with him. It's choosing not to take his pain personal, but instead understanding that his fight ain't with you—it's with his own demons.

But listen close—this don't mean you become his emotional punching bag. Nah. This ain't about tolerating disrespect or losing yourself trying to save him. **A real Queen knows how to love with compassion AND keep her boundaries solid.** That's the real strength, baby girl, knowing when to offer that gentle touch, that empathetic gaze, that quiet comfort, and at the same time she knows when to say enough is enough.

"You see a Queen's Tru colors when her dude's down bad. And a King? You'll see his loyalty when he's sitting on top of the world."

The Architecture of a Queen's Words: Building Blocks of Trust

Let me say that again for the ones in the back: *Compassion with boundaries.*

You remind him who he is, not by nagging, but by *believing*. By speaking life into him when the world tryna bury him. By having faith when he's too tired to have faith for himself. By being soft in a world that told him he gotta be hard 24/7.

And when he rise up? When he get back in his power? A Tru King gon' remember who was there, not just in body, but in spirit. He gon' know you didn't just love the man—*you helped rebuild the King.*

That's rare. That's sacred. That's the kind of compassion that makes a man never look at another woman the same again, 'cause she ain't out here to belittle him, to tear him down with harsh words, to cut him with that sharp tongue, or to diminish his spirit with sarcasm. Nah. That's weak energy, that's what insecure folks do, the ones who don't know their own power. A real Queen? She builds him up, brick by glorious brick. Her words ain't weapons she throws around carelessly to inflict pain or to prove a point, to win an argument at the expense of his soul. **Her words are medicine, a soothing balm that heals those unseen wounds, repairs the cracks in his spirit, and strengthens his very essence.** Her voice is the one that reminds him of his inherent greatness, whispers encouragement when he doubts himself, speaks life into his wildest dreams, and reminds him of the potential he holds. She understands the profound, almost spiritual power of her tongue, how it can either crush a man's spirit into dust or uplift him to unimaginable heights, inspiring him to conquer mountains.

She got that profound wisdom, that street smarts combined with soul intuition, to know precisely when to push him, when to challenge him to step up, to be better, to reach for that next level in his hustle, his character, his life. But she also got that profound grace, that deep discernment, to know when to just wrap him in comfort, when to simply listen without judgment, giving him the sacred space to process his thoughts, his fears, his triumphs. She knows when to offer that unwavering presence, that silent support that speaks volumes. Compassion, in its truest form, ain't blind; it's intelligent. It don't excuse no sorry behavior, no disrespect, no foul play, no crossing of boundaries. But it knows how to address it, how to call him higher, how to inspire accountability without being straight-up cruel or disrespectfully tearing him down in public or private. It's about leading him towards the light of recovery, towards growth, towards self-improvement, towards accountability, not just beating him down in the darkness of his mistakes, leaving him hopeless. It's about inspiring growth, not just pointing out flaws. It's about seeing the potential, not just the past.

His Rock, His Unwavering Harbor: The Core of His Kingdom

She celebrates his victories, whether they're massive triumphs that make headlines or just those small, quiet wins that only he truly understands, the personal battles he's overcome. She's his biggest fan, his loyal hype-woman, amplifying his successes, making him feel like the absolute King he is, worthy of all his achievements. And when he takes a fall? When the world knocks him down hard, when his plans go sideways, when he stumbles over his own feet, or when adversity strikes? She ain't kicking him while he's down, or looking at someone else, searching for a quick exit, a greener pasture. She's the one who stands firm, unwavering, rooted in her commitment. She's the one who strengthens him, helps him dust himself off, reminds him of his inherent resilience, and helps him get back on his feet, stronger than before. Her presence isn't a war zone, it ain't another source of stress or anxiety; it's that **safe harbor** he can always retreat to, where he can finally drop his guard, shed his armor, exhale deeply, and just be his authentic self, vulnerable and whole, without judgment. This is where he recharges his spirit, where he finds his Tru peace, and where he remembers who he truly is, beyond the roles he plays.

Now, don't you ever get it twisted, baby girl. Compassion ain't no weakness. It's not a flaw in your armor; it's the very foundation of your power. In fact, it's the most profoundly powerful feminine force known to man, capable of moving even the hardest of men, the most broken souls, to become better versions of themselves, to reach for a higher purpose, to unlock their own potential. And only a real Queen, a woman deeply rooted in her self-worth and confidence, a woman who knows her value, knows how to wield that power with grace, with understanding, and with a whole lotta genuine, unconditional love. Remember that, baby girl. Your compassion, wielded with wisdom and intention, can be his salvation, the very catalyst for his transformation. It can be the cornerstone of the profound, enduring kingdom you build together.

The Unseen Power of Compassion: Building Empires (Expanded)

Aight, you feeling that heart connection now? Let's really dig deeper into this compassion thing, 'cause it's not just a nice emotion; it's the absolute cornerstone of Tru Queen status, the bedrock of a lasting bond. It ain't just a fleeting feeling; it's a profound way of seeing the world, a profound way of being, especially with your man, who looks to you for that unique kind of energy.

Think about it, shawty. That man you with? He's out there dealing with all kinds of unseen pressures, battling demons you might not even know about, the kind that lurk in the shadows of his mind, just like I mentioned before. The world ain't always a kind place. Listen baby girl, You see this world? Its loud, Its tough, and sometimes it feels like you gotta be hard to make it. They'll tell you that compassion is soft, that'll get you stepped on. They're wrong. Dead Wrong!

This thing we call compassion? It ain't some flimsy feeling. Its a damn superpower, a force they don't even see coming. Think about it. When you truly see someone, their hustle, their hurt, their heart… that's when you truly connect. That's when the walls crumble. And that connection? That's the bricks and mortar of any real empires are built with.

And a real Queen? She's deeply attuned to his needs, even the unspoken ones, the ones he might not even realize he has. She knows precisely when to offer a strong shoulder to lean on, when to just listen without judgment, giving him the sacred space to process his thoughts, his fears, his triumphs, his doubts. She knows when to offer that gentle nudge in the right direction, a whisper of encouragement that inspires him towards his highest self. She celebrates his victories like they're her own, amplifying his successes, building up his confidence after he faces setbacks, when the world knocks him down, when his plans go sideways, or when adversity strikes hard? She's his rock, his unwavering support, the one who reminds him of his inherent strength and helps him rise again, stronger, wiser, more resilient than before. Her presence ain't a source of more conflict, more drama; it's a sanctuary.

Don't get it twisted, Compassion ain't about being a doormat or excusing every little thing he does wrong. Nah. Tru compassion has that deep, intelligent wisdom. The strength to understand, and to feel with someone, and still stand your ground. It sees the flaws, it acknowledges the mistakes, it addresses the shortcomings that need to be worked on, but it approaches them with understanding, with a genuine desire to heal and to build, not to simply tear down or punish. It takes a real strong woman, a woman deeply secure in her own power, her own worth, to be truly compassionate, to open her heart and offer that kind of unwavering, profound support. It's a feminine power that can soften even the most hardened heart, inspire a man to be better than he ever thought he could be, to reach for a higher purpose, to unlock potential he didn't even know he possessed. It's about speaking truth with love, addressing issues with kindness and respect, not with bitterness, or resentment. It's also about knowing that lifting others doesn't dim your own light, it makes the whole damn room brighter. And when you wield that compassion with grace, with genuine understanding, and with that whole lotta authentic, deep-rooted love? You ain't just his woman; you become his anchor, his confidante, his best friend, the Queen of his heart and his home. Remember that. That's a power that goes deeper than any argument or demand. It's the power to truly connect, soul to soul, and to build a lasting kingdom together, a legacy that will stand the test of time, an empire built on respect and genuine love.

The Wisdom of the Queen's Touch: Discerning the Authentic Need

What you just heard about compassion? That ain't no fairy tale. It's the real deal, straight up. It's the wisdom passed down from Queens who built empires, who understood the Tru source of their influence.

For you, baby girl, that kindness you got inside, that empathetic spirit, that ability to feel deeply and understand? That ain't soft. That's your **steel**, your Tru strength, your resilience. It takes guts to care, to truly connect, to open your heart, especially when the world ain't always kind back, when it tries to make you hard and cynical. You're tapping into your real feminine self with a powerful confidence when you lead with that. But when you offer that genuine support, that deep understanding, that unwavering belief in him? It's like throwing a lifeline in rough waters, pulling him to safety, building a bond of trust that runs bone-deep, that nothing can shake.

A real man? A man who truly deserves a Queen, who understands value, who is ready to build? He gonna remember that. In a world where so many feel invisible, that's a powerful thing. Loyalty ain't bought, it's earned through respect and understanding. Those who lead with iron fist, they might get a quick result, sure. That's a shaky foundation. One wrong move, one crack, and the whole thing can crumble. But an Empire built on compassion? That's built on respect and trust? He's gonna go extra mile for you. Not because he has to, but because he wants to. He'll believe in what you're building together. He ain't gonna see that as weakness. He's gonna recognize the incredible strength it takes to be that open, that supportive, that genuinely loving, that profoundly understanding. It can transform a dude, make him wanna step up and be worthy of that kind of profound, unwavering love. Most of these females out here get hurt 'cause they're tapping into their Tru feminine self from an insecure place, from a place of desperation or a need for validation, and offering it to the bums, the low-level players who don't recognize real value, who just use it and abuse it making Tru Queens to throw down her crown and forget who she is. So know the difference, baby girl, **be discerning**, and always move from a secured place, from a place of deep self-respect and knowing your inherent worth. Don't cast your pearls before swine.

The Echo of a Queen's Heart: Legacy Beyond Self

And when you move with that compassion, not looking for praise, not doing it for the recognition, not seeking validation from him, but just keeping it real, keeping it authentic, keeping it rooted in who you truly are? You become his rock. The one he trusts implicitly, the one he leans on when the weight of the world gets too heavy, the one he knows has his back, no matter what storms roll in, no matter what battles he faces. You ain't just a woman in his life; you become the **foundation of everything you build together**, the very ground upon which your shared future rests. That ain't about yelling or bossing around or playing petty games. It's about connecting deep, heart to heart, soul to soul, and building something so solid it can last through generations, a testament to Tru partnership. Remember that power, baby girl. It's a kingdom-builder. It's how Tru Queens reign. You feel that, really feel that in your bones. Consider the ripple effect. Your compassion doesn't just heal him; it teaches him. It becomes a blueprint for how *he* should treat others, how he should carry himself. And through him, you're influencing a wider circle, perhaps even a future family. You're building a legacy of empathy and strength that transcends your immediate relationship. This is the ultimate power move, the Tru mark of a Queen: to inspire transformation not just in her partner, but in the very world around her, one compassionate, discerning act at a time. It's an investment in a future where genuine connection, strength, and unwavering support are the currency. That's the depth of your influence, baby girl.

And that heart you offered him is gold dipped in understanding. Compassion was the opening move. And the next? Next rule is about claiming what's yours , locking it down with confidence that shines and love that binds… and yeah, maybe a little bit of that Royal sauce to keep things spicy. It's about showing him that you left the keys to the gate by the door and you ain't sweating about him leaving, 'cause the confidence you carry? It's a fortress, and the love you're dealing? it ain't a leash, it's a magnetic pull. Your whole Queen vibe will be screaming 'It ain't a threat, It's a promise' without you saying a damn word. It's a promise that he'll never step a foot inside your kingdom ever again once he leave.

The Way She Moves: Compassion for the World, Boundaries for Herself

Just in case you're still wondering, let's get one thing straight: compassion don't mean you're soft. It don't mean you let folks walk all over you, play you, or drain your energy till you ain't got nothing left. Real compassion? That's gangster. That's strength in silence. That's knowing your power and choosing to move with love, not ego. You've mastered compassion with your man — that deep, soul-rooted love that sees him, holds him, lifts him. But a **Tru Queen's compassion don't stop there**. It's how she **moves through the whole damn world**. What I mean is, this Queen energy you rocking? It ain't meant just for your man. Nah. That compassion? That power? That heart of yours? It's meant for **everybody** you cross paths with. Family, friends, strangers — not for them, but for *her*. Because when you stay solid in love, you never lose yourself to the haters and their negative energy. From the cashier with the tired eyes, to the friend that's low-key struggling but fronting like they're good, to the stranger that tests your patience in traffic. You ain't just a Queen to your King — you're **the embodiment of Royalty** in every room you step into. A Tru Queen should carry that with *everybody*.

But here's the flip side — and don't miss this: compassion don't come without **Boundaries and I'll get into Boundaries deep in the later chapters, but for now I wanna lay this down for you so that you can walk on the streets lessons that's coming**. So check it, just 'cause you got a good heart don't mean you let people abuse it. That ain't love — that's self-destruction. You gotta know when to show love and when to step back. When to forgive and when to let go. When to be soft and when to be steel. This ain't about being nice just to get stepped on. **Real compassion** is when you move with love, but you ain't no fool. You see through the BS, but you don't let it make you bitter. That's strength. That's **Street Knowledge**. That's the kind of presence that makes people check themselves before they even think about crossing the line. **Compassion ain't weakness. Compassion ain't permission. Compassion ain't silence in the face of disrespect. Which also means, that** in the streets, you see people — really see 'em — but you don't let 'em play you. It means you move with intention, with empathy, but also with fire. You can hug someone with one hand and hold the crown with another. You can love hard without playing yourself. You can be kind without kissing ass. You can forgive without forgetting the lesson. Your compassion is a reflection of your strength, not your tolerance for nonsense.

So when people come at you with shady vibes, backhanded compliments, manipulation, or just straight-up chaos — you don't gotta match that energy. **You rise with grace, shut it down with calm, and move like the Royalty you are.** You don't need to convince anyone of your value. You just show it. You just *be* it.

Let the world know through your actions that screams:

> *"I love deep. I move with compassion. But I don't play with small time energy."*

Because when your boundaries are solid, your heart can stay open without leaking out everywhere. You don't gotta harden up to survive — you just gotta **discern who's worthy of your softness.**

The streets might call it "cold," but a Queen knows — that's just discipline. That's love with wisdom. That's heart with heat.

Rule #4: Lock It with Confidence and Love – The Key to the Kingdom

Aight, Princess. This ain't just the last rule —
this is the damn key to the kingdom.
This how you lock it down —
not with flimsy chains of insecurity or desperate tactics,
but with something way more powerful.
Something that echoes in his spirit, shakes his core, and makes him say:
"This the one."

Feel this. This is something serious,
so *pay attention* and *absorb it.*
You might think this sounds like the last chapter —
you might be saying,
"Didn't we just talk about compassion?"
Well… you right — but not quite.

There's more to it. That's why I gotta break it down to you like this.

See, *compassion* is about holding space.
It's about *understanding*, *healing*, and *protecting his peace*.
That's where you meet him when he's broken,
when he can't see himself,
when life got him on the ropes.
You there like a sanctuary. That's Rule #3.

But Rule #4? This ain't about holding him.
This is about claiming him.

This is that *undeniable, soul-rooted love* mixed with *Queen-level confidence* that don't ask for the throne —
it commands it.
It's when you step into your full power, knowing what you bring, and you bring it *unapologetically*.
This ain't about just loving him through the storm.
This is about making sure he don't even *want* to go nowhere else —
not mentally, not emotionally, not spiritually.

Let's be real.
There's women who'll give him compassion,
and there's women who'll give him love.
But the one who gives both *and* backs it with confidence?
She's unforgettable.
She don't chase.
She *attracts*.
She don't beg.
She *blesses*.
She don't demand attention.
She commands presence.

When you love him from a place of wholeness, not lack —
when your confidence says, *"I know who I am, and I know what I deserve,"*
he feels that in his bones.
You ain't trying to prove your worth —
you're showing it through how you move,
how you treat yourself,
how you pour into him *without losing yourself*.

That's what makes a man *locked in*.

It's that rare combo —
soft heart, steel spine.
It's love that says,

"I choose you, but I don't need to lose me to keep you."

That's power.

You ain't afraid of his potential.
You ain't intimidated by his greatness.
You *speak life* into it and then show him
you belong next to it —
not behind it, not beneath it, and not above it
but right there beside it.

And don't get it twisted —
this ain't about being cocky or cold.
This is about being centered.
You know your love is a gift,
not a lifeline.
You don't throw it at anyone hoping to be chosen.
You offer it like Royalty —
and a real one gon' recognize the crown.

So while compassion holds him,
love and confidence lock him.
This chapter ain't about healing.
It's about claiming, anchoring, solidifying.
This is what turns a man's attention from the world
to you — and only you.

You become the home he didn't know he was searching for.
You become the standard.
You become the answer to the prayer
he was too tired or too proud to even speak out loud.

That's what this chapter is.

So step into it bold.
Step into it radiant.
Lock it with confidence.
Seal it with love.
Because when you do?

He don't just stay.
He builds with you.

To keep a **real one**—a man of substance and vision, the kind who is building an empire or steering his own ship—you cannot be out here chasing shadows or begging for scraps of attention. That is a low-level game, like playing checkers when he is thinking chess. it is a quick fix with an illusion of power, leaving you empty like a bag of chips after one bite.

Nah, the real play? It is about being that **undeniable force**, a magnetic pull he cannot resist. **You are** that rare frequency his spirit naturally tunes into, like a classic vinyl record spinning in a world full of digital noise. **You are** the vibe he cannot forget, the kind that sticks in his soul like a favorite ink on skin. That energy he cannot find anywhere else on this entire planet, making every other woman just a blur. **You are** becoming the **rare groove**, the timeless melody in a world full of static and superficial noise, a symphony he is always reaching to hear.

There are plenty of women out here who can snag a man, sure. They know how to turn heads with a look, a laugh, a curve, a quick spark. **They are** masters at playing the game, flashing fake smiles, offering quick thrills, and laying on surface-level charm. It is like a cheap chain, all flash, no real weight.

But the **real mastery**? The **Tru artistry**? The crown **you are** wearing high and undeniable? That is knowing how to **hold his heart**. It is understanding the blueprint to build a connection so deep, so authentic, that it becomes unbreakable, like a foundation poured in concrete. It is the kind of bond that can weather any storm, any hurricane life throws at it.

A **Tru Queen** is not on her knees, begging for attention or validation. She is not performing, putting on a circus act just to keep a man's eyes on her. She does not manipulate. She does not coerce. She locks him in with something way deeper: her unshakable **self-respect**, a fortress nobody can breach. She has a mind that truly understands life and love, seeing through the smoke and mirrors. And that raw, unapologetic **confidence**? It is shining from the inside out like a beacon, a lighthouse guiding his ship through the darkest nights.

She is not checking left and right, comparing her divine shine to another woman's flickering light. Hell nah. That kind of insecurity is for the ones who do not know their own light, who are still lost in the dark. She knows, deep in her bones, that **she is a limited edition**. A masterpiece forged from her own journey, painted in her own colors, on her own canvas, a unique piece of art that cannot be replicated.

But peep this—she also knows that knowing her worth is not a license to be rude, arrogant, or cold. That is just fronting. Her **loyalty**? It is locked tight—a fortress built on trust, honor, and commitment, strong as iron gates. But her **standards**? **They are** sky-high, reaching for the stars. Not because **she is** being picky or playing games, but because **she is** built different. She is crafted with patience, sharpened by discipline, and guided by a clear vision of what Tru love is supposed to look like—not a fairytale, but a real partnership.

She is giving her love freely, authentically, like a pure stream flowing—but only to a man who has genuinely earned it. A man who has proven he can stand **beside her** as an equal, not trying to be above her like a King on a throne, and certainly not dragging her down like dead weight for the rest of her life. He has to be on her level, walking the same path. She does not live in fear of getting burned, because she knows her worth is not tied to any man's choices or flimsy promises. Her value does not fluctuate with somebody else's loyalty, like stocks on a bad market day.

And even with all that power, that undeniable strength? She is keeping her **softness**. She is staying feminine, nurturing, radiant, a Tru rose in concrete—but, like I said before, never, ever becoming a damn doormat for anyone to walk over. Her confidence is not loud, it is not screaming for attention in the streets. It is that **quiet storm**—brewing in her eyes like distant thunder, anchored deep in her gut, felt in the room before she even speaks a word.

That silent, powerful confidence is telling her man, without a single whisper: "**You are not** here because I need you to complete me, like a missing puzzle piece. **You are** here because out of every soul on this entire planet, every single face in the crowd—**I chose you**." And that choice? That is **power**. That is how you lock his heart: not with fear, not with force, not with manipulative games, but with **love and confidence that does not flinch**, solid as bedrock. With her undeniable **presence**. With her unwavering **purpose**. With a vibe he cannot escape—because **it is real**, as real as the air he breathes. This is not about just holding space when he is broken; this is about making him never want to let go, even when he is whole and standing tall. That is the difference. And that, my baby girl, is the key. The key to the Kingdom that you're gonna build with a Tru King.

Love with Wisdom, Not Games: The Queen's Approach

She loves with a woman's deep, intuitive wisdom, not a girl's petty games or manipulative tactics. There's no unnecessary drama, no throwing tantrums like a spoiled brat, no playing those weak, manipulative hot-and-cold moves to test his loyalty. Just that steady, unwavering devotion, that profound feminine strength that wraps around a man's spirit and makes him feel like he finally found his peace, his Tru home base, his sanctuary from the chaos. It's the kind of love that builds empires, nurtures souls, and inspires greatness, not the kind that burns them to the ground with volatility.

See that girl? She ain't faking the funk. She's keeping it 💯, staying Tru to her authentic self and respecting who she is, down to her core. That's the first rule of the game: **know thyself, so you can respect and honor thyself**.

- **Emotionally?** Think of it like she's building a fortress around her heart. Not a prison to keep love out, but a powerful, impenetrable stronghold to make damn sure only the real ones, the worthy ones, can get in and reside there. That resilience, that profound ability to bounce back from setbacks, to weather storms, to cultivate inner peace? That's straight-up strength, the kind that can't be bought or sold.
- **Mentally?** She ain't letting her mind get rusty or complacent. She's always reading the streets, learning new plays, studying the game, expanding her knowledge, getting smarter every damn day. That continuous growth, that relentless pursuit

of wisdom, that expanding of her horizons? That's her power move, her intellectual hustle.
- **Physically?** She ain't just dressing up for show, for external validation. She's taking care of herself, honoring her temple, 'cause that's her right, her health, her vitality. Her body's her ride through this life, and she's treating it like gold, nourishing it, moving it, respecting it, and loving it. That self-respect, that deep self-care? That shines brighter than any diamond.

Bottom line? She's always **leveling up**. Always getting better, always evolving, not just to impress some dude or outshine another female, but 'cause that fire inside her, the one that forged her crown, that built-in drive for growth, won't let her stay still, won't let her settle for anything less than her full potential. That hunger to grow, to evolve, to become more? That's her engine, her internal combustion, and she taking her Tru King with her.

Remember this, baby girl. Stay Tru to your essence, build your inner strength, keep learning, respect yourself fiercely, and always chase that inner fire. That's how you become the Queen of your own damn world, truly sovereign.

Her Presence: The Ultimate Sanctuary

And her presence? It creates a damn **sanctuary**. A man can go out there and battle the wolves, face all kinds of demons, navigate the ruthless concrete jungle, the corporate battlefields, the personal struggles. But when he's with her, when he steps into her aura, her space? He can finally breathe. He feels safe, he feels truly seen, acknowledged, understood, and he feels that profound fire igniting inside him to be a better man, to rise to her level, to be worthy of that kind of connection. Her energy, her very essence, is his damn refuge in the storm, his compass and a lighthouse to navigate through the disruptive seas, onto the safe shore.

Keeping a man ain't about constantly trying to prove you are worthy, constantly performing, constantly seeking his validation. It's about **being worthy**, knowing your value down to your core, genuinely, without ever needing to explain it, without ever needing to seek nobody's damn approval, because it emanates from you. And a woman who operates from that core of self-love and unshakable confidence? She ain't losing sleep worrying about losing love. Truth is, she *is* love. She embodies it. She brings that profound peace, that unwavering support, that genuine understanding, and that pure, unadulterated connection.

Okay, so think about it like this: that inner peace you got brewing inside you, that quiet strength, that serene confidence, that's the most valuable stash anyone could ever find in this noisy, chaotic world. It ain't about the bling or the loud display; it's that quiet strength, that deep knowing of who you are, what you bring to the table. When a real dude, a man of substance and discernment, stumbles upon that, when he truly experiences that level of peace and genuine connection from you, it's like hitting triple 7s, finding that one thing he's been searching for his whole life without even consciously knowing it. He ain't gonna walk away from that kind of treasure. He's gonna hold onto it tight, like it's the last breath he'll ever take, like it's the key to everything good and stable in his life.

You being that peace, that calm in the storm, that unwavering light, that's what makes you unforgettable, irreplaceable. It ain't about playing games or trying to be someone you're not for him. It's about owning your authentic power, that quiet confidence that shines from the inside out, illuminating his world. A man with real vision, the kind who's looking for something deeper than just the surface, he's gonna recognize that genuine connection, that profound gift. He's not gonna let that slip through his fingers. He's gonna cherish it like his most prized possession, protect it from anything that could harm it, and build his whole world around that solid foundation you provide.

When you radiate that kind of energy, that authentic Queen vibe, it ain't about manipulation or begging for attention. It's about the undeniable force of your spirit, the magnetic pull of your genuine self. It's like a powerful magnet, drawing in what's real and pushing away the fakes, the shallow connections. That's the kind of legacy you build, a connection based on something real and lasting, a bond forged in mutual respect and profound love. That's how you truly reign in his heart, not through force, not through demand, but through the sheer, irresistible power of who you are. That's how you move, baby girl.

You ain't gonna trap him with flimsy nets of neediness, of emotional dependence. Nah, you building a fortress of self-worth so strong, so impenetrable, the very walls whisper "respect" with every breeze that passes by. Your confidence ain't a cheap perfume that fades after a few hours, a fleeting scent that disappears with the rain. It's the deep, earthy scent of ancient redwood, rooted and unshakable, reaching for the sky without apology, standing tall through any storm. When you step into his world, it ain't no soft dawn creeping in, a subtle change he might overlook. It's the full-force, undeniable crack of daybreak over a midnight sea. Blindsiding the darkness, making everything else fade into a shadow, 'cause your light, your essence, is the only damn thing that truly matters, the only thing that commands his attention.

And love? Don't get it twisted, it ain't a soft pillow he can just nap on, a comfortable convenience. It's the bedrock beneath that fortress. It's the relentless river that carves through stone, smoothing the rough edges of his soul, shaping him, refining him. You see his cracks, not as flaws to be fixed or exploited, but as valleys where your understanding, your compassion, your healing touch can flow freely. You ain't his mama, coddling his boo-boos, enabling weakness. You his compass in the wilderness, pointing him towards his own Tru north, towards his highest potential, even when the path gets thorny, even when he gets lost.

You ain't trying to clip his wings, baby girl. You the wind beneath 'em, the powerful current that lifts him higher than he ever thought he could soar, helping him touch the sky. You his sanctuary in a world full of noise, the quiet melody that soothes his restless spirit, quiets his mind. When he feels that unwavering belief in his potential, when he basks in the warmth of your genuine affection, when he experiences that profound peace you bring, he ain't looking for no other shore, no other harbor. He's home. Locked in by the unbreakable chains of mutual respect and a love that burns with a confident, eternal flame. Think of it like this. He's out there on the open water. Other women might offer him a quick stop, temporary port for supplies, but you? You ain't just no Got-Damn port, a shore, or a light house. You the whole damn Island. You ain't building no cage with your love. You're the safe harbor where his anchor digs deep and holds tight. Now, if that fool decides to drop anchor at some raggedy, temporary port for supplies, even though you filled up his whole damn ship with goods? That ain't a man worth your breath. You are a Queen who's crown is forged by a fire inside your belly and Tru Respect, Tru Compassion, Tru Love and Confidence as gem pieces on that crown. You ain't begging for ships to stay docked where it don't belong. You grab your Royal scissors and cut those ties clean. Let him drift. Your shores is too valuable for ships that don't know their Tru north.

So, let your inner Queen rise like the tide, powerful and undeniable. Let your confidence be the crown you wear every single day, with regal dignity. And let your love be the unbreakable bond that ties his heart to yours, not out of obligation, not out of fear, but out of a deep, soul-level knowing that he's finally found his Tru north in you, his ultimate destination. You got the power, girl. Now use it wisely, with purpose and with grace.

Wisdom from the OGs: Timeless Truths

Aight, now that we've laid down the blueprint for Queenly conduct, check these quotes from the legends themselves, 'cause each one is vibing with the essence of these rules, timeless wisdom from the streets and beyond.

- **El-Hajj Malik el-Shabazz (Malcolm X): "If you have no respect for yourself, you can't respect others."** This one hits straight at the heart of Rule #1: Be Respectful. Malcolm understood that Tru respect starts from within. You gotta value yourself, know your worth, before you can truly recognize and honor the value in yourself and others. It ain't about weakness; it's about self-awareness, inner strength, and integrity.

- **Tupac Shakur: "Real Kings and Queens don't flaunt their wealth; they walk in silence and know their worth."** This resonates deeply with Rule #2: Be Modest. Pac knew that Tru power doesn't need to shout, doesn't need external validation or flashy displays. It's in that quiet confidence, that inner knowing of your immense value without the need for constant display or boasting. Just like a real Queen carries herself with a regal humility, her power felt, not announced.
- **Tupac Shakur: "Real recognize Real"** This quote carries the spirit of Rule #3: Treat Him with Compassion. In the context of relationship, this quote calls for genuine understanding and acceptance. It suggests that a Tru partner who truly see her man, see beyond his facade, acknowledges his struggles. It implies a compassion that comes from truly knowing and understanding someone at their core, especially during their battles fought in the dark.
- **The Notorious B.I.G: "Stay far from timid, only make moves when your heart's in it, and live the phrase 'sky's the limit."** This quote speaks directly to Rule #4 Lock it with Confidence and love. Confidence, intentionality, and knowing your worth—living bold, with heart and purpose, just like a Queen who knows she's the prize, not the pursuer. It's about not moving out of fear or desperation, but from a place of inner strength, self-assurance, and genuine desire.

Yeah, that's the real talk I'd lay down for my shawty, the wisdom I'd instill in my young Queen. But best believe, I'm keeping that iron close for any of these lowlife Simps and suckas trying to run a play on her, trying to disrespect her, trying to take advantage. Forget that noise. This world's full of snakes with no damn conscience, slithering around, preying on the innocent and the young, trying to dim that Queen's light. I hope they sip on "The Antidote" – that real wisdom, that self-respect, that confidence – before they end up with a lead poison. Facts!

Aight, listen up, family. We've been on a real journey, digging deep into detaching from snakes that drains you, by knowing your damn value, and with that W.A.S mentality. What it means to rock that crown with Respect, Modesty, Compassion, Love and Confidence. We've laid down some serious blueprints for building that unbreakable connection, that undeniable vibe. Now, as we roll up on this final section, get ready to seal the deal, to truly fortify the empire you're building, whether it's with your King, your Queen, your Tribe, or just within yourself

Laced in Love, Locked in Loyalty

Chelsea didn't chase spotlights —
She was the fire that made 'em burn brighter.
Moved like prophecy in motion — smooth, sharp, unbothered.
She didn't raise her voice.
She raised standards.
And when she stepped in a room, even clocks held their breath.
Her silence? Not fear — **it was command.**
Steel wrapped in elegance. Grace with a backbone.

She didn't dress like royalty.
She bled it.
Not from diamonds or titles —
But from every scar she stitched shut with poise.
She wasn't shaped by luxury.
She was carved by loss.
Made of midnights, made it through hell, still glowed like holy.

Her story didn't lull babies to sleep —
It woke women from nightmares.
A war hymn in stilettos and hoodies.
And even the strongest break sometimes.
Even warriors get ambushed.
His name?
Dante.

Rule #1: Respect the Real

The community center sat in the hood like a **temple built from survival.**
Faded bricks. Fist-painted murals of the fallen and the rising.
Broken swings creaked outside like ghosts singing lullabies of second chances.

Inside?
The scent of bleach, cocoa butter, and unfinished business.
Laughter in the gym.
Arguments over spades in the back.
Kids holding basketballs and burdens too heavy for their age.

And at the center of it all?
Chelsea.

Bun tight. Clipboard loaded like a weapon.
Eyes sharp, movements precise.
She wasn't just staff —
She was the spine of the building.
The reason it didn't crumble under city budget cuts and forgotten promises.
She saved kids with curriculum and presence.
Tutored Malik through GED night sweats.
Got Marisol a crib and a crib for her baby.
She didn't clock out.
She clocked in for the forgotten.

And next to her?
Khalil.
Low-key like thunder before it hits.
Book-smart, street-hardened, emotionally lethal.
Didn't talk much, but when he did?
The air took notes.
A man who read peace like scripture,
and held Chelsea like she was sacred ground.

They weren't just lovers.
They were sanctuary.
Didn't call each other "bae."
They called each other *purpose*.
Until the devil walked in wearing cologne and cuff-links.

Dante.

Pulled up in a Benz with "4CHANGE" on the plates.
Suit loud, ego louder.
Smile slick enough to sell rain in a flood.
He strolled in like he owned the air.

That day, the community showed up deep.
Grant hearing in session.
City funds on the line.
Chelsea by Mama Rose's side — the OG of the block.
Silver hair, cane tapping out wisdom like Morse code.

Mama was speaking truth, rooted in pain,
when Dante cut in like static on a soul record.
"Look, ma'am," he interrupted, fake grin sharp.
"We don't need emotional speeches.
We need data. Metrics. Real results."
He turned to the crowd like he was on stage.
"No offense, but leadership don't come from bedtime stories."

The room froze.
Even the ceiling fan stopped spinning.
Even the toddlers paused mid-juice box.

Chelsea stood.
Heels cracking the floor like thunder.
Didn't flinch.
Didn't rattle off her degrees or her receipts.
She walked slow — a calm storm.
Kneeling beside Mama Rose like a soldier before a queen.

"Mama," she said, voice like velvet steel,
"your words *are* the blueprint. Without them, there's nothing to build."

Then she rose.

And turned.
To **him.**
No words.

Just that look.
That look that made grown men remember their manners.

She didn't blink.
Didn't snarl.
Just stared with a silence so loud,
it echoed through the marrow of his bones.

Dante choked on his own confidence.
Sweat bloomed behind his collar.
He stuttered. Fumbled.
Looked around for backup.

Khalil?

Just posted in the corner.
Arms crossed. Eyes calm.
He ain't need to move.
Because Chelsea had already flipped the table **with poise and presence alone.**

That day, the whole block got reminded:
You don't disrespect soil you ain't bled for.
You don't interrupt wisdom with spreadsheets.
You don't try to outshine a crown **you ain't earned.**

Respect the Real — or get exiled by it.

Rule #2: Be Modest

Weeks later, the city launched a youth leadership competition.
The prize? Funding and control of a pilot program.
And just like that — the sharks circled.

Dante came dressed for cameras, not community.
Campaign signs, buttons, business cards, a whole street team chanting his name.
"Make Youths Great Again." he called it. Flashy. Filtered. Fake.

Chelsea?
She moved like smoke. Quiet. Purposeful. Real.

She didn't sell dreams. She sowed them.
Early mornings mopping the gym after overnight floods.
Evenings mentoring girls with ankle monitors and poetry dreams.

Khalil watched her in awe, the way she carried burdens
like blessings.
She never asked for credit — just outcomes.

The final presentation was held at City Hall.
Chandeliers. Marble floors. Politicians with forced smiles.

Dante brought graphs and charts.
PowerPoint transitions. A speech full of buzzwords.

Then Chelsea stepped up.
No slides. No graphics. Just a worn blue folder.

She opened it.

"These are letters," she said. "From kids. From mothers. From men who got out and didn't go back."

She looked out into the crowd.

"Devon learned to read here.
Kayla stopped skipping school here.
Marcus stopped selling dope because he started coaching ball here."

Her voice didn't rise — it *resonated*.

"This ain't about numbers. It's about *names*.
We don't build futures with slogans and fake promises.
We build them with dignity."

Silence. Then a slow, rising clap from the mayor himself.

He pointed toward Chelsea.

"You walk it. The position's yours."

Dante blinked like someone had erased his hard drive.

Chelsea?
She just nodded once.
No grin. No mic drop. Just purpose.

Because real ones don't chase applause — they chase legacy while practicing modesty.

They are neither bullies nor doormats. Tru Royalties.

Rule #3: Master the Code of Compassion
It was raining heavy that Thursday.
The kind of storm that soaks straight through your soul.

Khalil came in late, hoodie dripping, jaw tight.
He looked like a man who'd fought a war and lost something he couldn't name.

He didn't speak.
Just dropped his keys, sat on the couch like gravity had betrayed him.

Chelsea was in the kitchen, steeping chamomile.
She saw him. Really saw him.
No small talk. No fake cheer.

She sat beside him, knee brushing his, placed her hand over his fist.

"I'm drowning," he whispered.
"Like I'm screaming inside a city that don't even know I exist.
I fix things, but nothing fixes me."

Chelsea looked at him, heart steady.

"You ain't broken," she said. "You're just heavy. And I got hands strong enough to help carry it."

She didn't try to fix him.
She just made space for him to be soft.

That was her power.

Compassion — not co-dependence.
Empathy — with edges.

She didn't pour into empty cups.
She didn't offer mediocre solutions. She *respected*.

And in that stillness, Khalil exhaled.
Not because she solved it — but because he finally felt
safe being seen.

Rule #4: Lock It with Confidence and Love

The day Khalil got the Atlanta call, the whole house felt like it was holding its breath.
Big opportunity. Bigger pay.
But risk?
Distance.

He stood by the front door, suitcase zipped, heart open and afraid.

"I don't wanna lose what we built," he confessed.

Chelsea didn't flinch.
She looked up from her tea. Walked over.

"You think distance is loss?" she asked.
She straightened his collar, her fingers gentle but firm.

"I'm not your leash, Khalil. I'm your launchpad."

He looked down.
She lifted his chin.

"You go build. I'll be building too.
This ain't teenage love.
This is *empire*."

He kissed her slow. Forehead. Then lips.

And as he walked out that door, she didn't cry.
Didn't beg.

Because what they had?
Wasn't held together by fear.

It was locked in loyalty.

Chelsea's Evolution

She checked the mirror not to fix her lipstick —
but to remember who the hell she was.

Not flawless. Not perfect.
But real. Rooted. Risen.

She had mastered the art of standing tall in soft skin.
Of loving wide without losing her voice.
Of being a Queen without asking for a crown.

Pain didn't define her.
It *refined* her.

Two Queens, Different Storms, Same Strength

One morning, just after sunrise, Chelsea was restocking the supply closet.
She turned — and froze.

There, by the lockers, stood Celeste.
No lashes. No gloss. No performance.

Just clarity in her eyes and strength in her posture.

"You new?" Chelsea asked, though she already knew.

Celeste smiled.
"Not new. Just finally back."

They stood there, silence doing all the talking.
Then Celeste said, "You ever get tired of folks mistaking kindness for weakness?"

Chelsea grinned, voice low.

"Only until I realized silence hits harder than any comeback."

They both laughed — not surface laughter, but gut-deep.
The kind that comes after surviving hell and choosing healing.

From that moment, they were sisters.
Two Queens. One mission.

Raising girls from rubble.
Building legacies from pain.

The Bigger Truth
While others chased clout, Chelsea chased purpose.
While they performed, she *produced*.
While they shouted, she *showed up*.

Now?
She wasn't alone.

Khalil held her heart in strong, loyal hands.
Celeste had risen from the ashes.
The community center wasn't a building anymore — it was a *kingdom*.

THE ANTIDOTE

Because when a Queen rise —
And a real King rides beside her?

The world watches.
And history takes notes.

They didn't just play the game.
They rewrote the rules.

SECTION 3

THE KINGDOM OF BOUNDARIES – FORTIFYING YOUR EMPIRE

Alright, Kings and Queens building empires brick by magnificent brick, listen up! You already know the crown you wear ain't just for show, ain't just for IG likes and comments. It signifies the power, the inherent worth, and the undeniable Royalty that flows through your veins. It's in your blood, your spirit. Now, if you're truly locking shields and building a kingdom together, something real and lasting, understanding your turf – your mental, emotional, and physical space – ain't a suggestion, it's straight-up **law**. It's the code you live by, the foundation of all genuine respect.

Before we lace up our boots and get down to the nitty-gritty of holding ground, of defending your sacred space, feel this vibe, let it truly resonate. This ain't about putting up walls to shut your partner out, to create distance or isolation. Nah, that's not the move. This is about building **strong foundations** so your kingdom, your partnership, your very being, can withstand any storms, any challenges, and any outside interferences. Think of it like this: even the most powerful armies, the most formidable empires, need well-defined borders to know exactly what they're protecting, where their influence ends, and where their undeniable strength truly lies. Without clear boundaries, you're just a free-for-all, vulnerable to invasion.

So, check the rhythm I'm laying down for this final, crucial section. We're talking about the very pillars that uphold your Royal decree:

- **Knowing Your Non-Negotiables:** What are those core values, those deeply ingrained dreams, those fundamental needs that are so deep in your spirit, so woven into your essence, they simply cannot be compromised? These are the sacred grounds of your individual kingdom, the bedrock of your integrity. You gotta know them cold, own them with every fiber of your being, and speak on them clearly, unapologetically. This ain't about being stubborn or inflexible; it's about knowing your truth, your authentic self, and standing firm in it.
- **Drawing the Line in the Sand:** Once you truly know your non-negotiables, you gotta be able to say, with clarity and conviction, "Yo, this far and no further." This ain't about starting fights or creating conflict; it's about setting clear expectations from the jump. It's about teaching folks how to treat you, what you'll accept, and what you distinctly won't. Silence ain't golden here; in the realm of boundaries, clarity is the real treasure, the currency of respect.
- **Protecting Your Peace:** Your mental and emotional space is your inner sanctuary, your personal temple. Don't let anyone just waltz in and start throwing shade, planting seeds of doubt, or dumping their toxic energy on your sacred ground. You got the undeniable right, the absolute duty, to guard

your peace fiercely, like a dragon guarding its gold. This might mean stepping back from certain draining conversations, limiting your exposure to negative or draining energy, or just needing some solo time to recharge your Royal batteries, to reconnect with your inner wisdom.

- **Respecting Their Territory:** Building a powerful kingdom together, a Tru partnership, means recognizing that your partner is also a sovereign ruler of their own domain, their own inner world. Their boundaries, their non-negotiables, their needs for space and respect, are just as valid and important as yours. This ain't a one-way street, a power trip where only your rules apply. It's about mutual respect and a profound understanding that two strong individuals make an even stronger kingdom when they honor each other's sacred space, when they see and respect the lines drawn by both King and the Queen.

- **Communicating Like Royalty:** When boundaries inevitably get tested, when they get crossed (and they will, 'cause we're all human, we all slip up), you gotta communicate like the King or Queen you truly are. Speak your truth with clarity and unwavering respect, not with accusations, blame, or emotional outbursts. Remember, the ultimate goal is to build understanding, to fortify the connection, not to tear down the castle, not to dismantle the trust you've worked so hard to build.

This ain't some fairytale where everything magically falls into place with a flick of the wrist. Building a powerful kingdom together, a partnership that endures, takes consistent work, brutal honesty, and the unwavering courage to hold your ground while fiercely respecting your partner's. You both bring unique power to the table, unique territories to protect. When you protect your individual territories with wisdom, with conviction, and communicate your needs with an open heart, that's when your shared kingdom truly thrives, expanding its reach and influence. Keep your crown high, your boundaries strong, and let's build something legendary, something that will be whispered about for generations. Feel that?

LINES IN THE CONCRETE

Aight, listen up, this one's for the soul,
The part of you that's done playing a fool's role.

It ain't love if it come with a leash,
insecurities tight like the grip on a piece.

You gave too much, now it's time to retreat,
Draw the line like paint on the street.

Don't reward disrespect, that's the law,
Every time you let it slide, you take a fall.

Guard your peace like vault in the trap,
'Cause snakes come smiling, ready to snap.

Don't overshare—keep some in the vault,
Too much spilling? That's your own damn fault.

Boundaries tight, like a fortress holding strong,
Not every detail needs to tag along.

Some things sacred, for your eyes alone,
Protect your story, claim what you've grown.

THE ANTIDOTE

Loose lips sink ships, that's the street decree,
Wisdom in silence, for all to see.

So guard your gold, the tales untold,
A little mystery keeps your power bold.

Some folks ain't real, they fishing for dirt,
Twist your truths 'til they leave you with hurt.

Don't react off emotions, just breathe and pause,
'Cause real Kings and Queens don't move with their paws.

Let 'em trip, let 'em bark, and let 'em bait,
You stay cool, stay smooth, and elevate.

And always—yeah, always—be willing to bounce,
If the vibe feel off, then don't let it count.

Boundaries ain't walls, they doors with locks,
Built so your peace ain't food for hawks.

Respect ain't begged, it's earned with grace,
Hold your ground, find the right place.

Know your worth, like the Royalty you are,
Building kingdoms, reaching for stars.

SUNNY MASTERPEACE

Draw your lines, let your truth be known,
Protect your peace, while you sit on the throne.

Communicate clear, like Kings and Queens do,
Strong boundaries built, forever Tru.

THE ANTIDOTE

Rule #1: Never Reward Disrespect

Aight, let's take that foundation we've been laying and build it out, make it resonate with that deep, undeniable truth. Listen up, Kings and Queens, gather 'round and hear the realness of this crucial commandment. Forget them dusty storybooks with weak Kings and Queens locked in towers, waiting for handouts. From the throne we are sitting on, side by side, not in some make-believe castle, but right here, in the thick of it, where the pavement's hot and loyalty's tested daily. This ain't no fairytale ending we stumbled into; this is real-life Royalty, carved out in the streets, earned through sweat, through sacrifice, and through unwavering respect for each other.

We ain't playing no childish games of one-upmanship or petty squabbles. We are running a kingdom, our kingdom, built on a foundation stronger than any stone, and the very first commandment, the bedrock of our reign, etched not just in stone but in our very souls, is this: **Never Reward Disrespect.**

See, every individual holding a piece of this crown, be it King or Queen, is holding it high because it was earned. You know your worth, deeply, profoundly. You ain't no fragile flower waiting to be plucked, no damsel or distressed duke hoping for a rescue. You are the force, a storm when you need to be, a shield for those you cherish. And your loyalty? That ain't some flimsy promise whispered in the dark. It's locked in tight, forged in fire, unbreakable for your partner, for your shared vision; that's the absolute truth. When you stand tall beside each other, you are a Tru sovereign in every sense of the word. You command respect not with a raised fist and empty threats, but with your integrity, your unwavering strength, and the justness in your heart. You are earning it, day in and day out, never having to beg for it. You are moving as one, a unified front, feel? That raw power, that unyielding resolve, is fueling your own determination, while your grace, your intuition, is sharpening your edge, guiding y'all with wisdom and understanding. You are a unit, a damn unbreakable alliance against whatever the world throws your way. United, you stand. Divided, you fall. Now go put that sh*t on the wall.

Let this truth resonate in your bones: within the dominion y'all forged, disrespect doesn't just fade away – it meets a brick wall. It earns no spotlight, receives no validation, gets absolutely nothing. Zero. Zilch. Nada. It's a dead end, a non-starter. Let no one dare to even consider crossing that line, to approach you with anything less than the respect due to Tru Royalty. And you gotta be united with it. If one of y'all is allowing the disrespect and the other one isn't, then it'll create a conflict, which can lead to handling the disrespect in a very destructive ways. Especially when these snakes can maneuver sideways with that venomous energy. Let them face an immediate and undeniable chill, a coldness that cuts deeper than any blade, an immediate withdrawal of your valuable presence as a united upfront. And understand this – that icy reception might be just the initial frost. Depending on the gravity, the sheer audacity of their disrespect, the consequences will escalate. We're talking a potential exile, a severing of connections so complete, it'll feel like they've been erased from your realm, from your consciousness. You are not about that weak, enabling nonsense of 'oh, they didn't mean it,' or 'let's just sweep it under the rug,' or 'let's just complain about it when they're not here.' Absolutely not. Words carry weight, yes, but actions? Actions are carving legacies. And disrespect? I'm not talking about that trivial error; I'm talking about that deliberate act against you and your kingdom. A heavy anchor you'll be forced to drag, far away from the strength and unity you embody. It brands them, isolates them, and ultimately ejects them from the powerful sphere you've cultivated. So let this be crystal clear: do not even be entertaining the thought of letting them bring that toxic energy into your realm. You have built this on a bedrock of unwavering respect, and you will be defending its integrity with every fiber of your being. Disrespect will find no reward in your court, only a swift and decisive consequence. That is the unwavering law of your powerful union as a united King and a Queen.

The Unbreakable Foundation

And for all you couples out there, the architects of your shared destinies, the builders of your own damn empires, listen to this truth etched in the very blueprint of lasting love: **do not let anyone – and I mean absolutely no one – get the twisted idea that they can walk all over you.** Not your so-called ride-or-die crew, not even those cool co-workers and neighbors, and certainly, never ever, never ever ever, from each other. From the jump, from the very first brick you are laying in your foundation, you gotta be setting that standard, clear and unyielding. You gotta be showing the world, and more importantly, showing each other, exactly what you stand for, what you will be tolerating, and what will be met with an unbreakable wall. Love might be the initial spark, the very ground upon which you build. Now Trust? That's the binding force, the mortar that's holding your individual strengths together. But respect? Yea, respect. That's the unshakable steel frame, the core integrity of your structure, the invisible force field that's protecting everything you're building from crumbling under pressure. Without that unwavering respect, the love will be withering, the trust will be eroding, and your empire? It'll be nothing but a house of cards waiting for the first strong wind to be blowing it all down. So stand tall, stand together, and let your actions be screaming: disrespect has no place here.

Don't Be Thirsty for Love

Another thing is, don't be so thirsty for love. Listen up, those out there that's seeking a genuine connection. Let this truth sink in like the Titanic, resonate within the chambers of your soul: don't be so damn parched for affection, so desperately craving validation, that you foolishly gulp down disrespect like it ain't even poison. Don't let that yearning for love, that primal desire to be cherished, be blinding you to the bitter taste of being belittled, of having your boundaries stomped on. Swallowing disrespect, pretending it doesn't burn, it doesn't hurt, it doesn't leave scars? You are only empowering the disrespect-er and diminishing your own damn spirit. You ain't some leftover scraps, understand? Don't let nobody be feeding you crumbs of love mixed with shade. Flip that script – but don't let that ego puff up like a cheap balloon neither. Don't get high off your own hype and start slinging disrespect like you Royalty. That ain't how a Boss moves; that's weak sauce hiding behind a tough front.

Real power ain't the loudest bark, ain't empty threats and putting folks down. Nah, real power? It's that silence that drops when you shut down that foolishness smooth and cold. It's standing solid after you draw that line, making it crystal clear what you ain't gonna be tolerating. It's that quiet fire inside, that unshakable belief in yourself that don't need no applause, no external validation. Real power is how you are carrying yourself, knowing your worth down to your bones, feel? It's that fierce promise you are making to yourself: ain't nobody gonna be dimming your shine or making you doubt who you are. Kings, Queens, let your actions be roaring – your respect ain't a request, it's a damn demand.

So stand tall, know what you are bringing to the table, and let that quiet strength be the loudest thing about you. Feel that? Aight, straight up. We ain't talking 'bout no backing down when disrespect comes knocking. And we sure ain't preaching no bully moves, throwing elbows and acting tough for nothing. That ain't the way of Tru Royalty. It's 'bout finding that balance, you feel me? Knowing your damn worth deep down. Standing firm in that truth, planted and unmovable when disrespect steps up. And it's moving through this world with a quiet fire, a confidence that don't need to shout, but screams "Go ahead and Try me" without saying a word.

So take this wisdom, straight from the Kings and his Queens, Panthers in power, united in respect: build your bond with a foundation so strong it can weather any storm. Keep that love genuine, pure, and untainted by the corrosive influence of disrespect. But let this be your unwavering anthem, the battle cry of your union: **'Never Reward Disrespect.'** Guard your inner peace fiercely, protect the sanctity of your shared space, and above all, protect your partnership, that sacred connection you've forged. That, my people, is the Tru Royal decree, the unbreakable law of your kingdom. No doubt.

The Code of the Crown: Beyond the Surface

Let's push this further, dig deeper into the concrete. This rule ain't just about what you *don't* do when disrespect hits; it's about what you *become* in the face of it. When someone slings that shade, when they try to step sideways on your integrity, they ain't just disrespecting you, they're testing the very fabric of your kingdom. They're probing for weakness, looking for a crack in the foundation you've poured with sweat and sacrifice. And if you reward that mess, even with a flicker of hesitation, a moment of doubt, you ain't just giving them a pass; you're handing them the keys to your damn fortress.

See, a Tru King or Queen moves with an undeniable aura, a silent force field that screams "access denied" to anything that ain't built on truth and respect, anyone that screams 'I am a poser' through their actions. This ain't about being confrontational, about getting loud or throwing hands. Nah. It's about that **unyielding still-**

ness, that cold, hard truth in your eyes that lets them know: "I see you. And that weak game you're running? It stops right here." It's the swift, surgical removal of toxic energy, like cutting out a cancer before it spreads through your whole operation. You don't negotiate with disrespect. You don't try to reason with it. You just make it obsolete in your space.

Think about the silence that follows a dropped mic. That's the energy you're channeling. When disrespect rears its ugly head, your response ain't a debate, it's a definitive statement. You don't owe explanations to those who refuse to see your worth. You don't owe your energy to those who seek to drain it. Your time, your peace, your presence – these are precious commodities, assets of your kingdom. To waste them on those who diminish you is a betrayal of your own crown, a theft from your own soul. You're not just setting a boundary; you're erecting an impenetrable wall, a declaration of self-worth that echoes through the streets louder than any shout.

And for the architects of your shared kingdom, for you couples forging that unbreakable bond: this rule becomes the very breath of your union. If you allow disrespect to fester between you, even the smallest crack, it's like a slow poison. It erodes the trust, tarnishes the intimacy, and turns your shared vision into a war zone. You have to be each other's fiercest protectors against this venom. When one of you faces disrespect, from *anyone*, the other stands as an immediate, unwavering force of support. It's a unified front, a shared code of honor. You communicate with clarity, not just in words, but in the iron-clad commitment to each other's dignity. You're building a legacy, not just for yourselves, but for the generations that follow. What blueprint are you leaving them? A structure riddled with cracks in weak spots or a fortress built on mutual reverence, strong and majestic, standing on top of a hill, which let people knows that, this building will be standing there for ages?

The Power of Knowing Your Value

And understand this deep in your gut: your value ain't up for public opinion. You ain't some product on a shelf, waiting for a price tag from the masses. Your worth is inherent, an unshakable truth that resides within you, a pure, uncut gem. When you chase validation, when you dilute your boundaries, you dim your own damn light. That desperation for connection, that thirst for love, can make you vulnerable to accepting crumbs when you deserve the whole damn feast. But a Tru sovereign doesn't beg; they command, not through arrogance, but through the magnetic pull of their self-respect.

The most powerful empires weren't built by individuals who tolerated being belittled. They were forged by those who understood that their strength lay in their unwavering standards, in their refusal to compromise on their core values. Your silence in the face of disrespect isn't weakness; it's a loaded weapon. It's the calm before the storm, the strategic pause that lets the other side know: "You just crossed a line. And there will be no reward for that."

This ain't about petty revenge or flexing your ego. This is about **sacred self-preservation**. It's about preserving your mental clarity, your emotional peace, and the purity of your spirit. When you reward disrespect, you're not just inviting more of it; you're telling yourself that you're not worthy of anything better. You're laying down the welcome mat for chaos. But when you cut it off, swiftly and definitively, you're sending a powerful message to the universe, and more importantly, to yourself: "My peace is non-negotiable.

My worth is undeniable. And my kingdom will only flourish in an atmosphere of genuine respect."

So hold that crown high. Let your stride be firm, your gaze steady. Let your actions be the loudest testament to your unwavering standard. Because when you truly embody this rule, when you absolutely **Never Reward Disrespect**, you're not just setting a boundary. You're laying down a legacy. You're building a kingdom where only genuine connection, earned loyalty, and profound mutual respect can thrive. And that, my people, is the Tru Royal way, the unbreakable law of your powerful union. No doubt.

Rule #2: Guard Your Peace (The Unshakable Fortress Within)

Yo, check it, Kings and Queens of your own damn thrones, architects of empires carved outta struggle and built with grit. When we talk about **Guarding Your Peace**, we ain't whispering sweet nothings in a dimly lit room. We talking protecting against anything that threatens that inner sanctum, that sacred space within you. Treat that stillness inside you like the rarest diamond, the most guarded secret known only to a chosen few, a blueprint for your very existence that cannot fall into enemy hands. This ain't no lucky break you just fall into, no winning scratch-off lottery ticket you stumbled upon. Nah, this is Fort Knox, locked down tighter than a federal reserve vault, and you, the Tru Rulers of your kingdom, are the sole guardians, standing vigilant against every damn intruder trying to steal your tranquility, to disrupt the very essence of your being. Your very existence, your damn destiny, the unfolding of your grand design – it all hinges on this, believe that. Word to the ancestors, this ain't no game; this is the ultimate strategic move. **"Ning jing zhi yuan."** That's the Chinese proverb which translates to **"Tranquility yields far-reaching vision."** It suggests that a calm and peaceful mind allows you to see things more clearly and plan for the future with greater wisdom. It's about the power of inner stillness for long-term perspective. So, in another words, a ruler without peace? They ain't a ruler at all. They a damn marionette, jerked around by every little drama, every fleeting emotion that whispers doubts or stirs up chaos. They jumpy, on edge, perpetually reactive to every damn string that's being pulled by unseen hands. That ain't leading, that ain't thriving; that's just existing in a constant, exhausting state of damn survival, putting on a grand, hollow show for the masses – the crew, the shorties, cats who wouldn't throw you a lifeline if you were drowning in the deepest struggle, only offering judgment from the shore. But peep this, there comes a **thunderclap moment**, a spiritual awakening so profound it shakes the very ground beneath your feet, when you gotta recognize the unfiltered, undeniable truth: your peace? That ain't some fluffy, touchy-feely notion; that's your **real damn power source**. Forget the frantic paper chase, the petty beefs that drain your spirit, the endless climb for superficial status, the fleeting pleasures that leave you emptier than before, the hollow hype that echoes like a barren tomb. **Peace.** That, my people, is the power you must protect, 'cause the silent roar that echoes through the deepest chambers of your soul, vibrating with an ancient power.

It is the unshakable bedrock your entire kingdom is built upon, the invisible but invincible foundation. Without it, the whole damn thing crumbles, your aspirations turn to dust, and your legacy fades to nothing. So guard it fiercely, like your damn life depends on it... 'cause in this game of life, it really does.

The Art of the Ghost Move

Alright, when you truly tap into that inner peace, when you harness its profound energy, your moves ain't no desperate Hail Marys flung blindly into the dark, hoping something sticks. Nah, they become **calculated chess maneuvers**, precise and ice-cold, each step deliberate, each decision a masterstroke. You ain't flinching at every little jab thrown your way, ain't wasting your precious breath explaining your grind to every envious soul hating from the sidelines, their eyes narrowed with resentment. You ain't tossing and turning at night when someone walks outta your life – let 'em go, allow the universe to clear your path. The kingdom ain't built on shaky foundations or flimsy attachments, remember? It's built on solidity and alignment. You drew the line and they crossed it. And you damn sure ain't begging for no cheap validation that costs you pieces of your damn soul, leaving you fragmented and diminished. Peace? That's the ultimate ghost move, the silent power play that leaves adversaries bewildered and observers captivated. You step into a room, and cats feel that inexplicable shift in the atmosphere, that heavy stillness that commands respect without a single word, without a single boast. When you finally choose to speak, they listen, not 'cause you the loudest mouth in the joint, but 'cause your silence carries the weight of thunder, the undeniable presence of a ruler in undisputed command, their words imbued with the gravity of undeniable truth, 'cause they got peace on their mind, bind by the crown forged by the fire from their bellies.

The Leaking Spirit: A Call to Action

But most of these cats out here? They bleeding their peace like a busted damn hydrant, that precious flow of vital energy gushing out, wasting it on every damn distraction, every fleeting impulse. Every impulsive text they fire off in a moment of emotional weakness, every petty squabble they dive headfirst into like a pool, every damn leech they let suck their energy dry with their endless demands and complaints, every guilt trip they swallow down like slow poison, every late-night gossip session draining their spirit with folks who wouldn't give 'em the time of day in the light, who would abandon them at the first sign of real trouble. Every single damn minute you spend explaining your worth to those who are too blind, too consumed by their own insecurities, to see it, is a drop of vital blood spilling from your spirit, a piece of your essence sacrificed. Over time, that constant, relentless leak leaves you hollowed out, a mere shell, just wearing the faded skin of a King or Queen who once had vibrant visions, dreams painted in vivid color that have now turned to ash, unrecognizable. Don't let that be your story. This is a battle for your soul. Guard your peace like your damn crown depends on it, because without it, the crown is just a heavy, meaningless ornament.

Can't lead no kingdom with a soul all cracked up and leaking light, constantly dimming under the weight of external chaos. And you damn sure can't earn that deep-down respect, that genuine reverence, when you always got your hand out, looking for some kinda quick fix from the outside 'cause you ain't ever dug deep and poured into your own damn well of self-sufficiency. Tru Kings and Queens?

They got a sixth sense for that weakness, that pervasive neediness. They can smell that desperation in the air – when your mind's a straight-up zoo, all the animals screaming and throwing their business everywhere, a blare of unresolved issues; when your time ain't locked down tighter than a bank vault, open season for anyone to steal it; when your personal space got no walls to keep the riff-raff out, allowing any low-vibration energy to infest your sanctuary; when your whole damn schedule bends and breaks for every little whim and breeze that blows through, making you a slave to external pressures. That ain't making 'em cherish your presence; that's making 'em feel like they holding the damn reins, steering your whole life like it's their joyride. And no self-respecting King or a Queen gonna ride shotgun for someone who needs directions every damn mile, who can't navigate his own damn path. Believe that!

Erecting the Force Field

So, let's break down this "guard your peace" code. It ain't about hiding in a damn bunker, retreating from the world. It's about throwing up an **impenetrable force field** against all the bullsh*t making yourself a **no-fly zone** for negativity and chaos, not 'cause you scared of a little rumble, but 'cause that's the damn blueprint for your ultimate victory, the master plan for your enduring reign. It's about looking dead in the eye at every single thing coming your way – that phone buzzing with drama, your whole damn crew and their endless baggage, your own self-sabotaging habits that whisper doubts, your jam-packed calendar screaming for your attention – and asking one cold-blooded, non-negotiable question: "Is this protecting my damn vibe, my inner sanctuary, the very core of my being, or is it slow-poisoning my spirit, eroding my strength?"

If it's poison? You gotta snatch that snake and cut off its head, right then and there. No dramatic goodbyes, no second chances for that toxic energy, no drawn-out farewells – just straight-up ghost mode, a decisive cut. You ain't wasting your precious breath arguing with fools who just wanna drag you down to their level, 'cause Kings and Queens who operate from a place of deep peace don't gotta explain their damn authority to the barking dogs on the sidelines, feel that! Their presence speaks volumes. You ain't chasing no fleeting illusions, no short-lived dreams, 'cause chasing keeps your eyes locked on yesterday's shadows, missing today's monumental blessings and tomorrow's grand opportunities. You ain't mindlessly scrolling through the digital wasteland, 'cause every single scroll is a conscious choice to numb your pain instead of building your future brick by brick, foundation by foundation. You ain't sleeping your life away, 'cause that's telling your soul your time ain't worth a dime, that your destiny can wait. And you damn sure ain't spilling your valuable energy talking to every body with nothing but static to offer; access to your mind, your time, your spirit? That's a privilege, an earned right, not freely given to just anyone. Treat it like the priceless treasure it is.

Peace is also laying down boundaries like **stone walls**, unyielding and unmovable, no damn explanations needed. You say no, and that's the decree, final and absolute, a period at the end of a sentence. You let texts sit if they from energy vampires, from ghost gatherings where drama's the main course, where negativity is served buffet-style. You let cats call you arrogant or cold 'cause they used to feast on your boundless availability, on your limitless patience. Let 'em miss you. Let 'em wonder what shifted. Let 'em gossip; while they running their mouths, caught in the quicksand of their own low vibrations, you building a kingdom where you choose who gets a key, who gains entry, not begging for love from folks who ain't even loving themselves, who can't even stand on their own two feet.

You rise with the sun, not 'cause it's a social media trend, but 'cause those quiet hours before the world wakes are your sacred ground, your fertile soil for growth. You read, not to look smart, but to expand your mind, to remember your problems ain't the damn universe, that wisdom lies beyond your immediate struggles. You walk your path solo when necessary, not 'cause you lonely, but 'cause peace walks hand-in-hand with the ruler who's solid on their own two, self-sufficient and complete. You train your temple, not for no mirror selfie or external validation, but 'cause discipline of the flesh is crucial for the unwavering strength of the spirit. And you keep your space clean, not for show, but 'cause chaos can't breed where order reigns, where clarity thrives.

The Untouchable Allure of Peace

Peace is power, profound and absolute, 'cause the ruler who commands their mind commands their world. The one who cannot be dragged into the mud of endless arguments, the quicksand of manufactured drama, the suffocating grip of guilt trips, the sudden chaos of fake emergencies, or the relentless pull of trivial distractions? **They are untouchable.** That's the allure, the unspoken desire that draws Tru allies. That's who genuine Bosses trust, who your loyal crew respects with an almost primal reverence, and who other powerful rulers look at and say, "That one's different. They move with an integrity that's rare."

Understand this: when someone throws emotional grenades, when they unleash their insecurities disguised as attacks, they might be trying to break you but they damn sure are testing your walls, seeing if your kingdom crumbles like I've mentioned before. When they spark a fire outta nowhere, ask loaded, manipulative questions, pull back to see your reaction, they ain't trying to hurt you in the way you think; they are searching for your core, for the vulnerability they can exploit. And if every time they poke, you flinch, if you react on impulse, there ain't no core, just damn reaction, a hollow response. But if you sit back, stay calm, let the silence hang heavy like a judgment, and respond only when you damn well choose to, with measured intent? You don't just guard your peace; you declare it to their hearts, you declare it straight to their mind with a few words that worth a thousand.

You wanna level up your life? Build a peace so strong it offends the chaotic so deep, it repels superficiality. A peace so real you don't even blink when they say you've changed, because you understand that growth is the only constant. A peace that draws in the right tribe, the genuine allies, and kicks out the energy drainers, the leeches who would feast on your light. And the profound irony in all this? When you live this way, when you embody this unwavering tranquility, everything you used to chase – validation, fleeting affection, empty praise, fleeting respect – starts bowing at your feet, 'cause now you the rare breed, the one who don't need the world's applause to know their worth, who is complete within themselves. That peace will heal your deepest scars, sharpen your instincts to an almost supernatural degree, reveal your Tru allies with crystalline clarity, teach you to love without losing yourself, without dissolving your boundaries, and build a foundation for your life that no storm, no betrayal, no loss, no earthly challenge can ever shake. Guard it like it's the Holy Grail, the very essence of your being. And once you taste that profound freedom, that liberation of the spirit, you'll never settle for the prison of chaos again. Eventually, they either align with your frequency, they rise to your level, or they exit your realm, unable to exist in your elevated atmosphere. Both are victories, profound and undeniable, 'cause the moment you sacrifice your peace to keep someone around, the moment you compromise your inner harmony for external acceptance, is the moment you lose yourself. And if you lose yourself, if the very essence of who you are starts to fade, ain't no love, no relationship, no material gain worth it, 'cause the ruler they loved, the Tru sovereign, is gone. What's the point of a crown if you ain't got no kingdom within to rule? So, The one who truly loves you ain't gon' let that happen. They are always gonna be there to straighten up your crown whenever it tilts to the side, or catch it if it ever falls, so that you don't have to worry and be at peace while you move on these streets, always knowing that they got your back. Be at peace, my Royalties.

Rule #3: Don't Share Too Much
(The Unveiling of Power)

Alright, Kings and Queens holding down your territories, this is a profound truth etched in the very fabric of enduring power, straight from the streets to the throne: sometimes, you gotta **zip your damn lips**. This ain't about putting on no fake front, no cheap disguise; it's about keeping that damn mystique thick, like the unyielding fog that rolls in before a major move, obscuring the path but hinting at massive power. Your Royal partner, the one who truly matters, they don't need the daily damn news report of your whole damn existence, every mundane thought, every fleeting emotion. Even when they say they do. What they truly craves, what truly ignites the embers of their spirit and keeps them captivated, is the damn depth of your soul, the vastness of your internal ocean, not to drown in every ripple of it day in and day out. they want to peel back those layers slow, deliberately, like uncovering ancient artifacts of immense value, not have you hand them the damn instruction manual to your entire being on day one. The minute you unleash the floodgates to every feeling, every insidious doubt that creeps into your dome, every scar you carry from battles fought, every grand dream you shout from the rooftops before it's manifested? You become something they weren't ready for – their fixer upper, a project requiring their emotional labor. And Kings and Queens, a real Kings and Queens, ain't falling for projects; they lock in with other Royals who carry their own weight with silent strength, who already have their blueprints drawn, their foundations laid, and are busy building.

Speak when that sh*t truly matters, when your words got weight and impact, when they land like a gavel striking truth, undeniable and resounding. Hold back enough to keep that magnetic pull strong, to maintain the gravitational force that keeps them orbiting your powerful presence. You been told your whole damn life to spill your guts, to be all "vulnerable," to bleed your soul on the pavement for the sake of shallow "connection." But let's keep it 💯 – where the hell has that gotten you? Did they hold you tighter when you laid bare all your anxieties, every tremor of your insecurity? Did they respect you more when you cried about life being a raw deal, about the unfairness of the game, begging for sympathy? Or did something subtle shift in their gaze, something unspoken, a quiet realization where they started seeing you not as their rock, their immovable pillar of strength, but as their damn emotional equal, just another soul grappling with the noise, another burden? And while that sounds all righteous and woke on paper, the street truth, the undeniable wisdom whispered by those who truly reign, is this: when you dump your whole emotional baggage on someone shoulders, they might offer comfort, they might even sympathize, but that primal craving for your strength, that intuitive need for your unwavering presence, starts to fade, replaced by a quiet sense of burden, a subtle resentment, and perhaps some level of regret. Can't dump your whole life on someone right away fam. You gotta let them learn that sh*t on their own term, on their own time. If you feel like they ain't never gonna learn and don't got time for you, they're not interested not even just a little bit, then bounce. Simple as that.

The Allure of the Unseen

There's a sacred distance, an almost mystical space, a powerful tension that keeps that flame burning hot between a King and his Queen, a dynamic charge that sparks enduring attraction and profound respect. Ain't 'bout lying or playing cold; it's 'bout that space between what your partner perceives you to be, the aura you project, and what they still ain't fully unlocked, the deeper layers yet to be discovered. That mystery, that unknown, the tantalizing promise of profound insights and hidden strengths yet to be revealed? That's the gasoline on the fire, the fuel that keeps the engines of desire roaring. That's what keeps them intrigued, what keeps them guessing, what sets you apart from every other Wannabes who lays their whole hand out from the get-go, hoping it'll make them stay, mistakenly believing that full, immediate disclosure equals deep, lasting connection. And when you kill that mystery, when you lay out every last secret, every facet of your being, every thought that flickers through your mind, you kill that damn tension. And when the tension dies, when that magnetic charge dissipates, so does that consuming desire, that fundamental pull that initially drew them to your unique light.

It ain't that you shouldn't have emotions. You ain't a robot; you bleed, you struggle, you got doubts that gnaw at your spirit in the quiet hours, moments of introspection. But the difference between a Royal who commands respect and a simp who's just tolerated, a place-holder in the game of life, is how they carries that weight, how they masters their inner world. A respected Royal feels deep, profoundly, their emotions running like powerful rivers, but they move with that fiery purpose, channeling their raw emotion into focused action, into building their empire. Royals never let their pain become their loved one's burden, a weight they have to shoulder, draining their own reserves. Royals don't weaponize their story for sympathy points, seeking solace in pity and weakness. They don't crumble under the weight of their past; they integrates that sh*t quietly, steadily, alone if they have to, forging it into impenetrable armor, transforming lead into gold.

When you overshare every detail too soon, you create emotional clutter. It's like dumping a whole damn landfill of unresolved issues at someone's door, suffocating them with your internal chaos. They don't know what the hell to do with all that baggage you just unloaded. It overwhelms them, and instead of feeling closer, instead of finding genuine intimacy, they starts feeling suffocated, trapped. Instead of respecting your perceived openness, they starts questioning your damn stability, your internal fortitude, your capacity to stand on your own two feet. And instead of leaning in, drawn by your strength and mystery, they instinctively starts backing the hell up, creating distance. Not 'cause they're cold-hearted, not because they lacks empathy, but 'cause instinctively, fundamentally, they want to connect with you step by step, to find solace in your strength, not become your therapist, constantly navigating your emotional storms. Patience is the key. Let your heart burn with patience and reap the reward of how you master that slow release of information.

The Power of the Unspoken Word

There's a reason the most respected Royals you know, the most influential figures in history, the Tru movers and shakers, rarely broadcast their whole damn life story. They give glimpses, potent, intriguing glimpses that hint at profound depth, not full documentaries available to the masses. They offer presents, moments of curated insight, profound truths dropped at the right time, not exhaustive explanations for every single thing. And they never chase connection through confession, never barter their vulnerability for affection, never seek to earn love through the revelation of weakness. They don't talk to be understood; they move with actions that demand respect, with a presence that speaks volumes without a single word, with a silent authority that commands attention. And that respect, that earned reverence, breeds an intimacy deeper and more profound than any words can conjure, a bond forged in shared understanding, unwavering admiration, and mutual growth.

You wanna level up your kingdom? Start treating your damn story like a damn vault, a closely guarded repository of profound experiences, of hard-won wisdom, not an open book left on the coffee table for any passerby to casually flip through. Let them earn access to those deeper chambers over time, through consistent demonstration of their worth, their loyalty, their genuine intent. Let them wonder what the hell makes you tick, what fires burn in your soul, what profound thoughts occupy your mind. Let them feel that silence, that magnetic absence of constant chatter, and choose to lean in closer when they got questions, drawn by the irresistible pull of the unknown. Answer just enough to keep them leaning in further, to fuel their curiosity, to deepen their investment. You ain't hiding; you're preserving that polarity, cultivating that depth, building that intrigue – the damn fuel that keeps that fire burning long after the first sparks fly, transforming fleeting attraction into an enduring blaze, a lasting legacy. Give them the actual fruit after you sow the seed and tend to its growth with patient, unwavering dedication, 'cause that's the evident proof of your hard work, the tangible result of your commitment. If you're impatient, if you rush the process, if you force the harvest, they will be tasting dirt, a bitter, unripe experience, instead of the sweetness of that fruit. Feel?

Most people mistake talking so damn much for a connection. They think if they just let the other person knows every crack in their armor, every single vulnerability, every past failure, they'll never leave and that screams manipulation. But the opposite is truth. People don't leave 'cause they don't know enough; they leaves 'cause you laid out the whole damn map on day one, and there was nothing left to explore, no mountains left to climb, no mysteries to unravel, no depths left to plumb. They stopped seeing you as a damn mountain to conquer, a formidable challenge to inspire growth; they starts seeing you as damn predictable, a solved puzzle that good to look at it for a second, a well-worn path. And predictability? That's the damn kryptonite to attraction, the silent killer of desire, the quicksand that swallows passion whole.

The Art of Strategic Revelation

This ain't 'bout manipulation; this is 'bout mastery, fam. **Emotional damn mastery**, the profound ability to govern your inner landscape. **Strategic vulnerability** – the kind of openness that comes with control, not bottling everything up until you explode in a chaotic outburst, but not bleeding out every damn wound either, turning yourself into a perpetual victim, demanding pity. You speak your truth when the time is right, when it serves a higher purpose, when it will create understanding, not just 'cause you feeling emotional and need to vent. You share your struggle when it serves the purpose of growth, of strengthening your bond through shared resilience, of inspiring deeper connection, not just 'cause you need a shoulder to cry on, an emotional crutch. You reveal your heart in doses that amplify your strength, that showcase your depth and capacity for feeling, not replace it with perceived weakness or fragility. I'm talking about with people who you've just started building a kingdom. Just in case if I wasn't clear. When you master that slow release, it makes people happy not burdened. Master it!

Another thing is you gotta stop trying to be damn relatable all the time, 'cause in your desperate attempt to be understood, to fit in, to appeal to the lowest common denominator, you soften that very edge, that unique sharpness, that regal distinction that made her look at you differently in the first place, that made you stand out from the crowd. You don't always gotta relate; you gotta radiate that Kingly or Queenly presence, that undeniable aura of self-possession and inner peace. You gotta hold your ground when disagreements arise, when opinions clash, when the world tries to sway you from your purpose. You gotta be okay with them not getting your whole damn picture right away, with not being fully understood at first glance, with the beautiful complexity of your being. That's okay! What's not okay is you tripping because you can't handle your own damn emotions, because you require constant external validation for your internal state, for your very existence. For them to not get you right away is what builds that damn tension, that magnetic pull, that irresistible attraction. That's what keeps them intrigued, keeps them wanting to know more, to delve deeper into your world. Your peace ain't a group therapy session where everyone's problems become your burden. Your mission ain't a committee meeting where every strategic move is debated and diluted by conflicting opinions. Your vision ain't up for damn debate every time you feel like spilling the beans. It gets diluted, watered down, losing its potency, its power. When you overshare your insecurities, they become weapons in the wrong hands, vulnerabilities for others to exploit, chinks in your armor. When you verbalize every fleeting feeling that bubbles up, you become a commentator on your own life, a passive observer, not a leader who dictates its direction.

Instead, practice the profound power of presence. Sit with your pain, truly feel it, acknowledge it, and then channel it directly into your daily tasks, into your grind, into building your empire. Use it as motivational fuel, transforming raw emotion into relentless drive, into unstoppable momentum. Journal your thoughts, process them internally, allowing clarity to emerge from the chaos. Channel that damn confusion into decisive action, into tangible progress, into moving forward. Build a damn fortress around your emotional world, so damn strong that only those who earn it, those who demonstrate Tru respect, unwavering loyalty, and genuine care, can enter its sacred space. And when they do, when they are granted access, you don't drown 'em in emotion; you invite 'em to witness your damn resilience, your ability to weather any storm and emerge stronger. You don't offload your burdens; you reveal the depths of your character, the strength of your spirit. You don't break down; you open up like a damn sunrise – slow, intentional, breathtakingly beautiful, illuminating the world with your light.

That's how you become unforgettable, not by how much information you dumped, not by the sheer volume of your confessions, but by how much damn weight you carried, how much emotional mastery you displayed, without making them carry it for you, without making them your emotional crutch. And the more you move like this, the more magnetic you become, 'cause now you're a damn rare breed, a Tru anomaly in a world full of open books and desperate pleas for attention. You ain't just a ruler with a damn story; you're a ruler with a damn center, a damn core of unshakable strength, a profound inner world that demands respect and intrigue. A ruler who doesn't just survive damn life, but navigate it with calm, with mystery, with the quiet power of someone who knows who they are and doesn't need the world's permission to be it. This is how you keep their attention, keep them captivated, forever drawn to your unfolding narrative. This is how you keep your damn edge sharp, always one step ahead. This is how you stay respected, not just in your kingdom, but in every room you step into, in every interaction. So, remember that oversharing kills attraction. Draw a line and know your boundary.

Side note for the Real ones
Don't Spill the 5 Crown Jewels

1. The Royal Family's Sacred Scroll
Your family's sacred scroll? That's your lineage, your foundation. Don't unroll that in the streets for every vulture to pick apart. Keep that drama locked down in the castle, where only the real OGs understand the struggle. Outsiders just gonna use that against you, trust.

2. The Blueprint of Your Dominion
You got the blueprint of your dominion? Big plans for the future, your strategies, your masterful moves, a vision for your kingdom? Keep that fire burning bright, but don't go blabbing every detail to every hustler on the block. Let your success be the thunder that announces your reign, not some whispered prophecy.

3. The Royal Treasury's Vault Code
When it comes to your Royal treasury's vault code, your stacks, your empire's wealth? That's strictly need-to-know, and they don't need to know! Protect your paper like it's the last diamond in the city. The less folks know about your bread, the less they can plot on it.

4. The Cracks in the Castle Walls
We all got 'em, weaknesses. But you ain't gotta put yours on blast for the world to exploit. Understand the cracks in the castle walls, work on 'em in the shadows, and turn 'em into strengths. Never let an enemy see your chink in the armor; let them only see the impenetrable fortress you're building.

5. Battles Beyond the Public Square

And when it comes to you and your partner, your ride-or-die, remember this: battles beyond the public square are for you alone. You got disagreements? That's natural, it happens. But you don't fight your wars on main street. You hash that out in the privacy of your castle, behind closed doors. Real Royalty handles their business with dignity, not for the entertainment of the masses. Keep that unity tight, and your kingdom will stand tall.

So remember, Kings and Queens, the power is in your hands, but it's also in what you keep locked down. Stay strategic, stay silent, and let your reign speak for itself. You got this.

Which leads me to this next chapter, which is all about that emotions baby... Lets get it!

Rule #4: Don't React with Emotions
(The Unconquerable Citadel)

This rule ain't just about playing it cool when the pressure drops; it's about **claiming absolute dominion over your damn soul, mastering your universe from the inside out.** This is the basic principle of your reign. **Don't React with Emotions.** This ain't 'bout having no damn feelings; that's robot talk, a hollow existence, and we ain't built like that, fam. We bleed, we feel, we burn. This is 'bout having **mastery over 'em**, a grip so tight they serve you, they become your most loyal subjects, instead of the other way around, where they're tyrants on your throne. A ruler who can't be moved emotionally at will by some toxic manipulative individuals, someone with a pleasant appearances, someone with a high status, someone with wealth. And by some trifling situation, by some fleeting thought, by the roaring noise of the crowd, by the whispers of doubt – that's a ruler who's starting to understand where their real strength comes from. It ain't from the muscles they flexes, it's 'cause they ain't no damn slave to what they feels in the moment. They feels it, acknowledges it, and then processes it, deep in the silent chambers of their wisdom, and then, and only then, they **chooses their response.** That's the game-changer, the sacred alchemy that transforms raw, volatile energy into refined, potent power.

The world out there, man, it's a constant factory of provocation, a damn matrix designed to keep you entangled in its chaos. It wants you to be reactive, jumpy, predictable, dancing to its frantic beat. Society's designed to push your buttons, to pull your strings, to get you to jump on command, to spill your guts on demand. Some people, they test for reactivity without even consciously knowing it, looking for that raw, unfiltered response, that immediate emotional feedback loop that tells them they've got you hooked. And some people, they live in damn reactivity, tossed around like a leaf in the wind by every little breeze of emotion, every passing mood, every external stimulus, every cheap shot. But the Kings, the Queens, who becomes **still in the storm**? The ones who finds their anchor in the eye of the hurricane, whose eyes are unblinking as the world spins? That's the one who dominates silently. You seen it play out on the block, in the boardroom, in your own crib – they throw a curve-ball. Maybe it's a sudden tone shift, a comment laced with bum ass sarcasm, an unexplained withdrawal of attention, a calculated coldness designed to destabilize. And right away, your stomach drops, your mind races, your damn words chase them like wind trying to hold onto water, desperate to grasp, to control, to explain, to justify. That right there? That's emotional reactivity. It's when your inner world, your peace, your very equilibrium, your sovereign domain, is at the mercy of their external damn behavior, their fleeting whims. And once they feels they got that kind of damn power over you, that ability to pull your strings and get you to dance, the whole damn dynamic starts to rot – slowly, deeply, damn permanently. That's when respect starts to evaporate like dew in the morning sun, leaving nothing but parched, barren ground.

The Unshakable Core: Your Internal Citadel

This is 'bout being a **sovereign, who uses emotional as their fuels to their success**. Sovereign – that's the keyword. It means you rule your own territory, your emotional landscape, with an iron will, and a clear vision. It's the profound ability to feel fully, to experience the whole spectrum of human emotion, from joy to sorrow, anger to bliss, without being ruled by what you damn feel, without letting it hijack your judgment or your actions. It's the kind of ruler who can stand in front of their partners while they test your limits, pushing boundaries, speaking disrespectful words, trying to provoke; a Boss questioning your damn value, challenging your competence publicly, trying to knock you off your square; or a stranger disrespecting you in plain sight, mocking your very presence – and not be moved from your damn frame, from your unshakable center, from your core integrity, from the very essence of your being.

You don't need to lash out, to raise your voice to match their chaos, to explain every damn thing like you're on trial, justifying your very existence, or plead for understanding from those who offer none, whose only goal is to diminish you. You need to remain rooted, unshaken in present moment. That's powerful without the damn noise, without the chaotic theatrics, without the desperate attempts to control external perceptions. Some potential partners test for this 'cause it tells 'em if you're real, if you're stable, if your strength is just for show or something deep down, something forged in the fires of self-mastery, a silent, undeniable force. And when you pass that test? When you hold your frame, when you remain unperturbed? They don't just relax; They melts, because they found the anchor in their storm, the calm they crave, the rock they can truly lean on. You become the living embodiment of stability in a volatile world, a beacon of Tru leadership.

But you can't fake this. You can't mimic calm while boiling underneath, seething with unmanaged emotions and suppressed rage. That's a trick you play on yourself, a weak facade that will eventually crack and shatter under pressure, and eventually, the truth leaks out, revealing your Tru, unmastered state. It starts deeper, with owning your triggers, facing the parts of you that flinch when someone disapproves, that panic when someone pulls away, that rush to defend when someone questions your motives or character, even when they're baseless accusations. You look those parts in the eye, acknowledge their existence, embrace them without judgment, and then you say, with the force of a thousand hearts, with the unwavering conviction of your sovereign will, "You don't bleed no more. Your power over me is revoked. I am the master here. My internal kingdom is impenetrable." You become intensely aware of your damn impulses, those automatic reactions that hijack your consciousness, and instead of obeying 'em like a puppet, you observe 'em. That's the space – the sacred space between stimulus and response, the fractional moment of conscious awareness before action. In that moment of conscious choice, that's where Tru Kings and Queens are born. That's where Tru power is forged, not in outward displays of aggression, but in silent, internal battles won, in the disciplined cultivation of your inner world, the relentless polishing of your soul.

The Alchemy of Self-Mastery: Turning Lead into Gold

This practice of emotional non-reactivity isn't just a defensive strategy; it's an active alchemy that transforms you from the inside out. You become a student of human nature, a quiet observer of the subtle currents beneath the surface, the unspoken intentions, the hidden agendas. You start seeing what others missed, the Tru motivations behind the chaos. You start hearing what's behind their words instead of just reacting to the words themselves, your memory become sharper so that you can recall events to check their lies, and to recall vocabularies from your dome and power to choose the right words against the storms. You starts understanding the deeper message, the underlying need or fear, the desperate plea for attention. You stop needing the last word, the ego boost of victory in a meaningless argument that drains your energy and tarnishes your spirit. You stop defending your character to people who ain't even qualified to judge it, whose opinions hold no weight in the vast, expanding territory of your kingdom. You start living like your attention is gold – 'cause it is, it's one of the most valuable currency of your life force, your focused energy, your mental real estate. And if someone wants access to it, if they want a piece of your peace, if they seek your presence, they better come correct, with respect, with genuine intent, and with value to offer, not to take.

This also profoundly changes how people respond to you. The ones who used to provoke you, who thrived on your reactions, who reveled in your emotional outbursts, get frustrated 'cause they can't move you no damn more. Their old tricks become useless, their manipulation tactics rendered powerless, their attempts to steal your energy foiled. They start questioning their own bum ass approach, their own toxic patterns, because your stillness reflects their own inner turmoil, forcing them to confront it. And the ones who respect genuine strength, who seek stability in a chaotic world, start gravitating toward you 'cause calm attracts clarity like peace attract happiness. And clarity attracts every thing chaos repels. You'll notice you talk less. Your words become precise, effective, each one carrying the weight of intentionality. You move slower, with deliberate intent, each step a conscious decision, a measured advance. You observe more, soaking in information, assessing the landscape, reading the subtle cues. You wait. You study. You no longer react to their changing moods, their unpredictable silence, their indirectness, their emotional storms, their attempts to create drama. Instead, you understand their damn emotions are their own, their own unique waves, part of their journey, and if you can be the container for those waves without drowning in 'em, without getting swept away by their current, they will trust you more than any damn person they ever known. Not 'cause you saved them, not 'cause you fixed them, but 'cause you didn't lose yourself by trying. You remained solid, a lighthouse in their emotional storm, unwavering and Tru. Know yourself so that you know what you can truly handle.

The Ultimate Superpower: Navigating Chaos with Purpose

In life? This is the damn superpower, the cheat code that will elevate you above most damn people, 'cause most people are slaves to their emotion, camouflaged as "passion," confused with authenticity, mistaken for strength. They fight battles that don't matter, draining their energy on pointless conflicts, chasing shadows in a labyrinth of their own making. They burn good bridges and not f#cked up bridges 'cause their ego was bruised, sacrificing future opportunities, loyal connections, and their own growth for fleeting pride. They chase arguments to defend fragile pride, constantly proving a point to no one but themselves, trapped in a cycle of exhausting reactivity. But you? You exit chaos like it's beneath you – 'cause it is, it's a lower vibration you refuse to engage. You don't get pulled in; you walk around it, above it, through it without contact.

Here's the twist, the Tru power move: When that emotional grenade lands at your feet, or the world tries to drag you into its frantic rhythm, you don't just *not react*. You recognize that the very *urgency* they're trying to impose is an illusion. You understand that every ounce of emotional energy they try to provoke is energy that could be building your damn empire, polishing your crown, strengthening your bloodline. So you don't just hold your peace; you **re-direct that energy, internalize it, and transform it into fuel.**

You'll walk into a meeting where your idea is questioned, your competence challenged, your vision doubted, and you'll smile, a subtle, confident smirk, not out of arrogance, but because you know their doubt is just misplaced energy. You won't argue; you'll let their words hang, and then you'll return to your blueprint, sharpening your plan, making your next move with even greater precision. You'll have a friend betray you, cut deep by their actions, and instead of retaliating, instead of seeking petty revenge that would only diminish your spirit, you'll disappear like oxygen from damn fire, leaving them with nothing but the aftermath of burn, no fuel for their destructive intent. Your absence will be louder than any shout. You'll hear rumors 'bout you, baseless whispers designed to undermine your reign, to tarnish your name, and you'll say nothing, because truth don't panic. It stands on its own, undeniable in its quiet power, waiting for its moment to reveal itself. You'll be ghosted, rejected, overlooked, faced with disappointment and setbacks that would crush lesser individuals, and you won't crumble; you'll rise – quietly, with damn purpose, using every perceived setback as fuel for your next ascent, a stepping stone to higher ground.

No damn emotional reactivity means you stop handing over the steering wheel of your life every time you feel something, every time an impulse strikes, every time someone tries to dictate your response. You stop living by their clock. You start choosing your direction with discipline, with intentionality, with sovereign purpose, guided by an inner compass that never wavers, calibrated to your highest vision. And that discipline? It builds your kingdom, one unshakable brick at a time, one firmly held boundary at a time, until your empire stands as a testament to your ultimate self-mastery, a monument to your unyielding will. This is the code of the unconquerable. This is the path to Tru, unassailable power. This is how you don't just survive the game, you *change* the whole damn system.

Rule #5: Be Willing to Walk Away (The Ultimate Leverage)

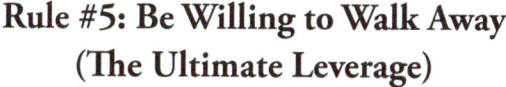

Listen up, fam. I'm laying down that detachment sh*t again, 'cause it is that damn important! That OG commandment, amplified and etched into your very bones: **don't you EVER waste your damn time**. Peep this, to all those out there striving for greatness, you might think you've stumbled upon Tru Royalty, or found your destined partner and ready to rule the kingdom together. But if your hustle ain't got the patience to really let the game I'm dropping on y'all to let it marinate, to truly absorb this wisdom, then this **detachment** sh*t is gonna be tougher then, pulling a wisdom tooth out with a plastic tweezers. So, listen close, because this right here is the damn truth, the real deal holy-field, straight from the street to the throne room: **always, ALWAYS be willing to bounce, to cut ties, to pivot.** Let that sink in like a stone in the deepest ocean, anchoring itself in your core. **Detachment ain't just a word, it's your damn lifeline.** It's the ultimate power play, the move that declares your independence to the universe. You ain't meant to be suffering while other take advantage of your sacrifices. You have the every right to pursuit happiness and be free in a responsible way.

Too many of my people out here getting stuck in the mud, bogged down, draining their spirit in dead-end gigs that suffocate their ambition, clinging to shrinking relationships that clip their damn wings, getting played by so-called friends who ain't got no respect for their grind or their peace. Why do they stay? **Fear.** That snake in the grass whispering venomous lies. Fear of rolling solo, fear of hitting reset, fear of the peanut gallery's gossip from the cheap seats, fear of the damn shadows that chase you when you step into the unknown. And all that fear? That's fertilizer for the poison that choke your damn growth, so here's the Antidote. The stronger those poison get, the smaller you become, until you're just a shadow of your former self, a mere echo of the King or Queen you were born to be. These dream thieves, these energy vampires, they grin in your face, and tell you, "Chill, it ain't that bad. Just stay put. It'll get better." And little by little, your vibrancy fades into the background – not just to everyone else, but you start losing sight of your own damn self, your own damn purpose, your own damn light.

Don't let that happen. Your time is precious, a finite resource. It's the one thing you can't get back, can't buy, can't borrow, right?. Your spirit is a raging fire, the very engine of your destiny; don't let nobody piss on it, don't let nobody extinguish that flame. Know your worth, feel it in your bones, that deep, unshakable conviction, and when something ain't feeding your soul, when it's weighing you down instead of lifting you up, when it's asking you to compromise your identity, you gotta have the G in you, the fortitude, that damn courage to say "Nah, I'm out." Walk away with your head held high, knowing you ain't settling for crumbs when you were born to feast at the Royal table. That ain't weakness, that's straight-up power. That's you reclaiming your throne, asserting your dominion over your own narrative. So remember to adopt the attitude of **"live by the boundaries, die as a legend."** "Live by the boundaries" ain't about being boxed in by someone else's playbook; it's about setting your own damn standards, the unbreakable laws you live by – your hustle, your loyalty, your grind, your integrity, your peace. You plant those seeds of discipline and watch them grow into an impenetrable forest of respect, a kingdom built on unyielding principles. And "die as a legend"? It's about living so fiercely, so authentically, so Tru to your damn code, that your impact echoes long after you move on. It's about every step you take, every move you make, leaving a mark that can't be erased by time or tide.

So rock that attitude like it's the freshest gear you own, tailored specifically for a Royalty. Walk with that fire in your chest, that internal furnace of purpose. See how the streets start to notice you, how opportunities start lining up, how the universe conspires to meet your unbreakable will. This ain't a game; it's your life, your damn story, and you're the sole author. Go out there and write a saga they'll be talking about for generations – write it without a single spoken word of boast. Write it with your own blood, sweat, and tears, etched into the very fabric of reality. You ain't just got this; you ARE this.

Now go make 'em remember your name by being the one who's willing to walk away from any damn thing that insults their soul. That person is terrifying. That person is damn magnetic 'cause they don't stay for comfort; they stay 'cause it aligns with their standards, with their damn destiny. And the moment it doesn't? Yeah, they're gone. And that absence, that dignified withdrawal, speaks volumes.

The Unspoken Language of Departure

This hits hard, especially in relationships, where the stakes feel highest, where emotions run deepest. A damaged partner senses that quick, that subtle shift in energy, that quiet conviction in your eyes. They know when you're staying 'cause you're addicted to their presence, desperate for validation, clinging to a comfort zone, versus when you're staying 'cause they bring peace, growth, and damn purpose into your world, truly aligning with your vision, elevating your spirit. The first type of individual, the "Simp," gets tested relentlessly; their boundaries pushed, their worth constantly questioned, their patience tried. The second type, "The Real," the sovereign? A damaged or an insecure partner watches themselves closely around them. They bring their best because they know you'll leave the second they stop respecting what you bring to the table, the moment the alignment cracks, the instant their actions disrespect your core. Now, that might not be how a Tru partner *should* be, operating from fear of loss, but it's a starting point, a necessary crucible for growth. This is where you lead, where you demonstrate that your love is not weakness. You show them not to be afraid of your strength, and that they need not to walk on eggshells 'round you, but rather to operate with integrity and respect. Your willingness to walk away frees them to be real, to rise to their own potential, knowing you only demand authenticity and mutual respect, not blind support and love. It allows them to step up, or step out.

Walking away ain't 'bout being damn heartless, a stone cold killer as I've reminded you many times before; it's 'bout being loyal to yourself above all else, loyal to the divine vision of who you're meant to be. It's 'bout saying, "I love you, but I love my values more. I love my peace more. I love the King or Queen I'm becoming more, and I will not compromise that sacred journey for anything or anyone." That kinda detachment ain't cold; it's divine. It frees you from begging for crumbs, from settling for less than you deserve, from accepting disrespect. It elevates your circle, it purifies your damn space, sending a clear, loud ringing message to the universe about your non-negotiables. It reminds you that nothing, no pleasure, no comfort, no affection, is worth keeping, if it costs you your identity, your integrity, and your soul.

And when you live like this? When you truly embody this rule, when it becomes woven into the very fabric of your being? People rise to your level, attracted by your undeniable presence, or they don't exist in your sphere. There ain't no middle ground, homie, no lukewarm territory. Your standard becomes the filter, the unyielding gatekeeper to your kingdom, allowing only what serves your highest good to enter. And over time, every damn thing left in your life reflects who you are at your highest, most powerful, most authentic, and most sovereign – not your most fearful, insecure, or desperate self.

You gotta become so secure in your self-worth, so grounded in your purpose, so clear in your vision, that you can walk away from pleasure, comfort, fleeting attention, superficial validation, and even damn love if it means protecting your mission, your destiny, your very essence. That's when you're truly dangerous – not to others in a physical sense, but to mediocrity, to co-dependence, to stagnation, to any chain that tries to cage you, to dim your light.

The Unwritten Chapter: After the Walk

And here's what most folks won't tell you, because either they really don't know, lost in the shallowness of the game, or they just greedy with the knowledge, clinging to it like an insecure dummy. The real growth, the profound transformation, the Tru ascension, happens **after you walk**. The strength, the clarity, the consistent expansion of your being – it don't come while you're holding on to that poisonous tree, clinging to what diminishes you, what keeps you bound; it comes in the silence that follows your final, courageous step away. In that space, in that courageous void, in that quiet solitude, you meet the next, most powerful version of yourself. The one who no longer tolerates chaos for the cure of loneliness. The one who no longer begs for scraps of attention. The one who no longer stays just to feel needed, to fill a void in others, to play a role that isn't Tru to their spirit.

Be willing to walk away from any damn thing that makes you forget who you are. Anyone that violates your boundaries, that disrespects your hustle, that attempts to derail your purpose, that tries to pull you back into the quicksand of their unmanaged life. And once you are truly willing to do that, once that conviction solidifies in your soul? You'll never beg, never chase, never tolerate disrespect again. The moment you choose self-respect and courage over false comfort, over the illusion of security, over the fear of the unknown, your life truly begins – not just your relationships, not just your confidence, but your entire damn life, my Royal people. The person you were is gone, shed like an old skin, left behind in the dust of your past, and the person you're becoming? That person don't chase no approval; they **builds standards**. They don't fold under pressure; they **sharpen in silence**. They don't seek to be understood; they **seeks to be undeniable**.

You were never meant to live on your damn knees for love, attention, or acceptance. You were meant to walk in power – quietly, calmly, with the unshakable knowledge of your inherent worth, your divine right to reign. Tru respect ain't something you demand; it's something you design through your actions, your standards, your unwavering adherence to your code, and your ultimate willingness to walk away.

If you felt that shift deep in your core? That reverberation in your very spirit, that ancient wisdom awakening within you? Then don't let it fade. Lock it in. This ain't the end; this is the start of a new era for you. A version of you that no longer tolerates being less than you were born to be. If this message struck something deep inside you, if it reminded you of the person you were always supposed to become? Then wake up and start respecting your damn self, be disciplined, and follow all those rules. Trust!

Love With Lines & Structure, Not Lies & Secrets

Enrique and Aaliyah weren't strangers to struggle — they came from a city where broken hearts were background noise, where trust was treated like a gamble, and loyalty was often mistaken for weakness. But they weren't building from the streets — they were building beyond them.

Their love wasn't some fairytale. It was forged in fire, polished through pain, and defined by discipline. See, Enrique and Aaliyah had learned something powerful: love without structure is chaos. And peace? That's not something you fall into — it's something you fight for.

This is how they built it — rule by rule.

Rule #1: Never Reward Disrespect

Their first spark hit on a rainy Thursday. Enrique had just gotten off a double shift at the garage, hoodie soaked, jaw clenched from the day. Aaliyah was walking out of the corner store with a bag of ginger tea and incense. They locked eyes at the crosswalk, both paused. No pickup lines, just presence. Real recognized real.

That flame carried them fast, but fire without boundaries scorches everything.

A month in, they had their first real argument. It started small — groceries. Who was picking them up. But it cracked open something deeper.

"You always gotta be right, huh?" Enrique barked, pacing the small kitchen of her apartment. "Just like every-damn-body else — always tryna control me."

He wasn't yelling. But his tone was jagged, sharp enough to bleed.

Aaliyah, in her gray sweats and bare feet, leaned against the counter. The scent of cinnamon tea lingered in the air, soft and sweet — nothing like the tension that now clouded the space.

Old Aaliyah would've clapped back — maybe thrown something, maybe matched his tone. But healed Aaliyah? She didn't flinch.

She looked him square in the eyes and spoke low, but clear: **"Enrique. That's not how we talk to each other. I don't reward disrespect — not from strangers, and not from you."** Her voice didn't rise, but it echoed.

"You mad? Fine. But don't cut me to feel better. I'm not your outlet."

He stopped mid-step, chest rising. The room went still. Then his shoulders sagged, and he rubbed his forehead like he was ashamed of his own voice.

"You right," he muttered. "That was foul. I'm sorry."

And in that quiet moment, respect grew. Not because they avoided conflict, but because they refused to use it as a weapon. Disrespect didn't get applause — it got checked.

Rule #2: Guard Your Peace

Aaliyah was a force behind the chair. Her salon station was more than mirrors and curlers — it was a pulpit, a therapist's couch, and a battle zone all in one.

Some days, the vibe was beautiful — women laughing, stories flowing, feminine joy on full display. Other days? It was war. Gossip flung like razors. Clients nitpicking. Co-workers throwing shade between smiles.

Aaliyah would come home wired, voice loud, retelling every messy moment.

"So I told Keisha — 'If you don't like how I trim edges, you can take that split-end energy somewhere else!'" She paced the living room like she was still in the salon, arms flying, rant on 10.

Enrique, sitting on the couch in sweats, tried to keep up. But his mind was tired. He'd just come from mentoring youth at the rec center, pouring himself out for kids with broken homes and empty eyes. He needed peace — not another fight from the outside world.

He waited until she paused for breath, then gently reached for her arm.

"Baby… pause. I hear you. I do. But right now… your noise is trying to steal my silence."

She blinked, lips parted, stunned.

"I need a second. Just an hour. Let me recharge so I can show up for you right."

Aaliyah crossed her arms. "So what — I gotta shut up now?"

"Nah," he said, calm but grounded. "You ain't too much. I just need to fill my tank so I don't start running on fumes around you."

She stood still. Then nodded slowly.

"I'll read," she whispered. "Come find me when you ready."

And later that night, after the silence had softened the edges of the day, he curled up beside her. No forced smiles. Just peace restored.

Because peace wasn't passive. It was mutual maintenance. And love without it? It was just noise.

Rule #3: Don't Share Too Much

Sunday mornings were sacred. They made pancakes from scratch. Marvin Gaye on the speaker. Sunlight pouring through the blinds like God's own spotlight.

Enrique had just fallen asleep on the couch after breakfast. Aaliyah, barefoot and grinning, picked up her phone. He was laid out — one hand on his chest, the other dangling off the cushion. Soft snores. Vulnerable. Beautiful.

She snapped the photo. Her finger hovered over Instagram.

"My peace. My home." she typed.

Then stopped.

She stared at the screen. Something felt off. The world didn't need this piece of him — not this one. She locked the phone.

Later that night, she brought it up.

"I almost posted that pic of you," she said, sitting across his lap.

He smirked. "The one where I look like I just saw Freddy Krueger in my dreams?"

"Exactly," she laughed. "But I didn't. Some moments gotta stay sacred."

He kissed her hand. "That's why I trust you. You know when to hold what's ours."

And it wasn't just pictures. It was privacy in general. One time, she started gossiping about a co-worker who got caught cheating.

Enrique didn't even flinch. Just kept chewing, then glanced up.

"You too royal to talk on peasants, baby."

That shut it down. Not with shame — but with elevation.

In a world addicted to oversharing, they found power in preservation. Not secrecy — sovereignty. Because not everything real needs to be revealed.

Rule #4: Don't React with Emotions

Money was tight. Bills were due. A payment from one of Enrique's contracts hadn't come through, and Aaliyah had just found out the rent went up.

They were standing in the kitchen, tension coiled like a spring.

"You said we had this covered!" she snapped, voice cracking with pressure.

"I *thought* we did," Enrique fired back, voice climbing.

Old wounds opened — childhoods filled with scarcity, with eviction notices taped to doors like threats. Trauma did what it always did — hijacked the moment.

Aaliyah clenched her fists. Her voice was ready to draw blood.

But then…

She remembered.

His words.

"Freedom ain't about geography. It's about emotional control."

She stepped back, took a long breath. Exhaled slow.

"Wait," she said, raising her hand like a traffic stop. "We're spiraling. I feel it. I'm about to say something I can't unsay."

Enrique paused, nostrils flaring. Then nodded.

"Let's both take five. Meet in the living room with cool heads."

They separated. Sat in different rooms. Let their triggers settle.

An hour later, they returned. No shouting. No scars. Just strategy.

Because calm wasn't weakness. It was warfare mastered.

Rule #5: Always Be Willing to Walk Away

The offer came on a Wednesday. Six figures. Full relocation. Prestige. But it came with a cost — 60-hour weeks, no vacation, toxic corporate culture, and a goodbye to everything Enrique was building in his city.

He came home, envelope in hand. "They want me in New York. Tomorrow."

Aaliyah looked up from her planner.

"That bag sound heavy," she said. "But what's it cost?"

Enrique was silent. He saw it already — the way the job would eat his time, devour his purpose, disconnect him from his community. And from her.

"If it robs your soul," Aaliyah said softly, "it's too expensive."

He exhaled, slow. "You're right."

He declined the offer.

Because success that demands you sacrifice your soul is just a shinier form of slavery.

The Return of Chaos

Sariah came back like trouble with lipstick. She had that magnetic energy — the kind that pulled you in before you remembered how much damage it caused.

She ran into Enrique at the gas station. Tight jeans. Fake smile.

"You still fine, Rique," she grinned. "You miss me?"

He smiled — out of courtesy, not curiosity.

"Nah. I'm allergic to drama now."

She didn't stop. DMs. Flirty comments. Showing up where she knew he'd be.

One message stood out:

"We had fire. I still think about it."

He looked at it. Then deleted it.

That night, he sat beside Aaliyah.

"Sariah's back. Tried to stir something."

She didn't flinch. Just asked, "You entertain it?"

He shook his head. "Didn't even respond. I protect our peace — always."

She leaned into him, whispered, "Thank you."

Grace Over Games

At a charity event, Sariah showed up. Showing all the curves. Intentions loud.

She found Enrique mid-convo. "Miss me yet?"

Before he could respond, Aaliyah appeared.

"Hey, babe. You introducing me?"

Sariah's face flickered. Aaliyah held out her hand with Queen-like calm.

"Pleasure," Sariah forced.

"I'm sure," Aaliyah replied. "But don't worry — I don't compete with memories."

They walked off hand-in-hand.

"Baby," Aaliyah whispered, "we earthquake-proof over here."

Final Words

In a city where love is tested daily, Enrique and Aaliyah built something unshakable.

Their peace wasn't luck — it was layered.

Their love wasn't loud — it was structured.

And their legacy? Built not just on passion… but on principles.

Because love without lines is a wildfire. But love with structure? That's the kind that lasts through storms

The Crown That Waited, Then Walked

Michael gave Denise five years.
Not five lazy years. Not half-effort, halfway love.
He gave her the kind of loyalty that could build a kingdom.
Showed up when it was hard. Loved her when she didn't
love herself.
Shared dreams, broke bread, paid bills, held her down when life
hit sideways.

They had memories woven into the walls —
movie nights on the couch with takeout and no heat,
arguments followed by apologies that sounded like promises,
plans made in whisper voices over pillow talk,
dreams birthed in bedrooms with more hope than furniture.

But lately?

The laughter went missing.
The vibe grew cold.
And the woman he once called home felt more like a stranger
holding a grudge.

Love didn't leave with a scream.
It leaked.
Word by word. Wound by wound.

Until Michael looked in the mirror one morning, saw a man he
barely recognized,
and asked himself the realest question of all:

"How long you gon' keep bleeding for somebody who don't even bring bandages?"

Rule #1: Never Reward Disrespect
Michael didn't want fame.
Didn't care for clicks or clout.
He was building something for the block —
a nonprofit with purpose, rooted in pain he once survived.
For the boys nobody checked on,
the ones left to fend for themselves in broken homes and harder streets.
Because he had been that boy.
Angry. Ignored. Invisible.

So now? He was becoming the man he once needed.

But Denise?
She treated his purpose like a phase.
"That little project again?" she'd scoff, lips twisted, eyes heavy with judgment.
"That's cute, baby. One day you'll get a real job."

Every time, he tried to hold his tone.
Tried to let love lead.
"This ain't charity, D — this is legacy. These kids need more than hope. They need structure, they need presence, they need to know they matter."
But she didn't hear him. Didn't try.
Just sipped her wine and shot down his mission like it was fiction.

"Michael, c'mon. You act like you Malcolm X. You ain't saving nobody."

And right there — in the echo of her laugh —
he learned that disrespect don't always slap you loud.
Sometimes it comes soft,
in a voice you used to love,
disguised as sarcasm.

She didn't raise her hand.
She lowered his worth.
Mocked what mattered.
Minimized what made him whole.

And for a while, he let it slide.
Let her jokes pile on top of his silence.
Told himself she'd understand *one day*.
But disrespect that gets tolerated?
Always mutates. Always multiplies.

He didn't raise his voice. Didn't make a scene.
He just started shifting.
Stopped explaining.
Stopped sharing.
Stopped handing out front-row seats to someone who only came to heckle.

Because the deepest kind of loyalty?
Isn't about staying.

It's about knowing when to stop **rewarding** someone
who keeps spitting on everything you're trying to build

Rule #2: Guard Your Peace
The apartment used to feel like sanctuary.
Now it felt like a setup.

Michael moved through it like he was dodging landmines.
Couldn't bring up the nonprofit, the boys, the events —
not without catching a stray.

One night, he came home glowing —
his latest workshop had been a breakthrough.
A young man who'd been on the edge gave him a hug and said,
"You're the first man who ever saw me."

He told Denise that story with pride in his voice.

She yawned and replied,
"You gonna write a children's book next?"

He said nothing.

But his heart took note.

The final straw came at a family dinner.

He mentioned a fundraising event, smiling as he spoke about new sponsors and volunteers.

Denise rolled her eyes in front of everyone.

"Oh, Lord. Another bake sale? You out here playing hero again for somebody else's kids?"

The table went still.
His brother dropped his fork.
His aunt stared into her greens like they had answers.

Michael didn't snap.
Didn't defend.

He just went still — the kind of still that means something's about to end.

Because real peace?
It's not quiet if you gotta fight for it every day.
Peace without respect is just tension on mute.

And Michael was done choking on silence.

Rule #3: Don't Share Too Much
After that dinner, Michael stopped opening up.

Not out of fear.
But out of *clarity*.

She had made it clear —
his purpose wasn't sacred in her hands.

But that wasn't all.

Denise loved to talk — *too much*.
Always had the tea, always had a story.
She'd air out other people's secrets like she was on a live podcast nobody asked for.

Sometimes, even her own family's affairs.

And Michael started wondering…

If she spills *everyone else's* **business like that —
how sacred is** *his*?

He noticed it all now.
How she giggled about her best friend's relationship drama to coworkers.
How she shared her brother's money problems, and her mother's unfaithfulness to her dad with strangers over brunch.
How her lips stay warmed up, while her heart stays cold.

And the more he watched, the more he pulled back.
Because if someone can't honor privacy,
they'll never protect your purpose.

So Michael locked the doors to his dreams.
No more late-night convos about the nonprofit.
No more letting her into the sacred rooms of his mind.
She had lost the right to access.

Because **some people only want a front-row seat to your downfall —**
not your rise.

Rule #4: Don't React with Emotions

She was mid-rant again one morning.
Something about him being "too emotional,"
about how she felt "drained being the only adult."

Michael stood in the kitchen folding a hoodie.

She didn't even notice that he had started packing.

"You're always the victim," she snapped.
"Maybe if you spent less time saving the neighborhood and more time being a man—"

But Michael didn't take the bait.

He just zipped the duffel bag.

Calm.

Silent.

Each folded shirt a declaration.
Each step back to himself a step toward peace.

He didn't raise his voice.

He let his absence say everything his presence had been trying to explain for years.

Rule #5: Always Be Willing to Walk Away
He stood in the doorway —
keys in one hand, truth in the other.

"Denise," he said softly,
"I can't do this anymore. You don't see me. You don't *value* what I'm about.
And I've already spent too much time proving my worth to someone committed to misunderstanding me."

She scoffed.
"You leaving over a dream? Over a charity project?"

He shook his head.

"I'm leaving because I refuse to lose *me* trying to hold on to *us*."

No tears.
No drama.

Just a King choosing his crown.

The Bigger Truth
The new apartment was smaller.
No shared photos. No familiar smells.
Just peace. **Sacred, steady, earned.**

Michael woke up early again —
no eggshells. No side-eyes. No sarcasm waiting behind
every sentence.

He prayed. He stretched. He worked. He smiled.
Not because life was perfect —
but because he finally stopped living in a space that required him
to dim his light just to survive.

The nonprofit grew.
He started speaking at schools.
Boys who had given up on themselves started standing taller.
Mothers thanked him. OGs respected him.

And when a young mentee asked him,
"Coach Mike, what made you start all this?"

Michael smiled. Looked out the window.
And said,
"Because I knew what it felt like to be unloved, unseen,
and unheard —
and I promised myself I'd never let another soul feel that
on my watch."

The Final Word
Michael didn't leave because he was weak.
He left because he finally understood:

THE ANTIDOTE

The loudest love is the one you give yourself.

He stopped rewarding disrespect.
He guarded his peace like a King guards his gates.
He made his mission sacred.
He moved in calm, not chaos.
And he walked away with dignity —
not because he gave up on love…

…but because he finally remembered he deserved *real* love.
Supportive. Steady. Silent when needed. Loud when necessary.

This wasn't a breakup.

This was a **return to the throne**.

Because the crown may wait…
but when it walks?

It walks with purpose.
With clarity.
And with **no need to look back**.

The Queen That Refused the Cage

Gabrielle and David had a love that started like a verse in a perfect poem—sweet, intoxicating, full of promise. But as her light grew brighter, his shadow grew darker. What started as admiration turned into envy, and what felt like destiny turned into a silent battle for control. This is the raw, unfiltered story of how a Queen broke the chains of control and reclaimed her crown—guided by the code of boundaries, the power of silence, and the unshakable truth of her voice. David was charming, passionate, and promised her the world. And when he looked at her in those early days, it was like she was the only woman on Earth — his muse, his goddess, his everything.

But David came with a storm cloud attached – a tempest of jealousy, control, and explosive anger that erupted whenever Gabrielle shone too brightly. His admiration turned territorial. His love turned to control.

Her career as a spoken-word artist was taking off — open mics turning into booked venues, videos of her performances going viral, women in the crowd crying because her words hit so deep. She was becoming a voice for the voiceless. But every success was met with David's storm.

Rule #1: Never Reward Disrespect

Gabrielle was soaring. Her spoken-word pieces were going viral. Colleges were calling. Protest stages were echoing with her truth. Women were wiping tears mid-set because her poems gave voice to what they'd buried for years.

She was becoming a symbol. A mirror. A movement.

And David?
The same man who once called her "Queen" —
now looked at her like a threat to his own relevance.
"Who were you talking to after the show?" he'd ask, teeth clenched.
"Why'd you wear that? You know how people look at you. You like that kind of attention?"

At first, Gabrielle pushed back. Tried to reason.
But over time, she adjusted.
Dialed it down.
Played it safe.
Not for her craft — for his comfort.

And that's the trap.
Disrespect rarely starts loud.
It creeps in sideways —
a guilt trip here, a cold shoulder there,
until you find yourself changing to please someone who's punishing your growth.
Her sets got shorter. Her style dimmed. Her voice softened.
She thought she was protecting the relationship —
but in reality, she was **rewarding the very behavior that was breaking her.**

What should she have done?
Draw the line.
Hold her ground.
Let him know — *"Your discomfort with my power isn't my problem to fix."*

Because every time you bend for disrespect,
you teach it to return.
And every time you stay silent,
you sign off on your own mistreatment.

But Gabi didn't leave.
Not yet.
She still believed love could overpower control.
Still hoped that maybe he'd see her heart and not just
his own shadow.

And that was the mistake.
Because when you reward disrespect with loyalty,
you teach a man that your boundaries are flexible.
You hand over your crown and call it "compromise."
You start bleeding for a love that don't even bring bandages.

She should've walked.
Boldly. Quietly. Completely.
Because the longer you stay where respect don't live,
the more you forget how to recognize your own worth.

But once a boundary's been broken, peace don't come easy.
Gabrielle didn't walk away that night — but something inside
her shifted.
She stopped trying to prove her worth to a man who was
threatened by it.
She started tiptoeing through her own life, guarding pieces of herself like fragile glass,

trying to keep the storm from spreading.
Because when you stay after repeated disrespect, survival mode kicks in.
And the next battle?
Ain't about love.
It's about protecting your **peace** in a war you should've already left.

Rule #2: Guard Your Peace
In the weeks that followed, Gabrielle stayed — but her spirit started moving.
She stopped explaining herself.
Stopped inviting him into her world just to watch him tear it down.
The home they shared still echoed with tension, but inside, she was building a new sanctuary — quiet, invisible, and hers alone.

She wrote late at night while he slept, pen gliding like a blade across paper.
Her journal became her shelter. Her poetry, her rebellion.
She lit candles when he left for work. Played music he hated.
Not to provoke him — to remember what it felt like to breathe freely.

David noticed the shift.
Her silence started to bother him more than her voice ever did.
"You barely talk to me anymore," he snapped one night.
"You act like a stranger in your own house."
But she just blinked, calm.

"I'm not a stranger," she said softly. "I'm just finally choosing silence over survival mode."

Because that's what peace is sometimes —
not fireworks, not big speeches.
It's the choice to stop explaining your soul to someone who keeps trying to shrink it.
It's moving slower, softer, deeper… until your spirit starts feeling safe again.

She hadn't packed yet.
Hadn't made any grand exit.
But she was reclaiming inches of herself every day —
a thought she didn't share,
a line she didn't cross,
a piece of her power she didn't offer for approval.

Because Gabrielle learned something crucial:
You can't keep watering a garden that someone walks through with muddy boots.
And peace?
Peace isn't passive.
It's something you *guard* like treasure —
especially when you're still sleeping next to the very chaos trying to steal it.

Rule #3: Don't Share Too Much

By now, Gabrielle had gone quiet —
but it wasn't the silence of fear.
It was the silence of strategy.

She stopped announcing her dreams.
Stopped offering her heart like a menu to someone who only came to criticize the meal.
She journaled in code.
Kept her phone close.
Left the house without saying where she was going,
came back with poems he'd never hear.

David could feel it.
The distance. The locked doors that used to swing wide.
And it ate at him.

David started noticing the silence.
Not just the kind that fills a room —
but the kind that means something's shifting beneath the surface.

"You still writing?" he asked one evening, watching her from the kitchen doorway.
She didn't look up. "Always."
"What about?"
She smiled without warmth. "Wouldn't you like to know."

The more he pried, the less she gave.
And the quieter she got, the louder his insecurity screamed.

"You always act like I'm the enemy now," he said one night, standing in the doorway while she folded laundry.
She didn't look up. "I don't act. I just move different."
"You used to tell me everything," he pushed, voice rising. "Now I don't even know who you are."
She met his eyes, calm as glass. "That's the point."

The more he demanded,
the more she disappeared into herself.
David started digging —
scrolling through her messages while she was in the shower,
asking friends what she'd been saying,
snooping through notebooks trying to decode her new poems.

But Gabrielle didn't give him anything worth finding.
Her real life now existed behind locked doors — mental, emotional, and spiritual.
A vault he no longer had the key to.

He tried guilt.
"You used to be an open book. What happened to *us*, Gabi?"
She tilted her head, tired of the act.
"You didn't read the pages when you had access. Now the book's closed."

One night, after one of her performances, she came home glowing —
not from the applause, but from the peace of being around people who truly saw her.

David was waiting in the living room, arms crossed.
"I saw the photos," he said flatly. "You hugged some dude after your set. You smiling all big now?"

Gabrielle didn't even pause.
"If you're looking for something to be mad about," she said, slipping off her coat,
"you'll always find it. But I'm done handing you the map
to my peace."

Because she had learned something heavy:
When a man starts using your openness as ammunition, silence becomes survival.
She wasn't being secretive.
She was being selective.
She wasn't hiding.
She was healing — away from eyes that didn't know how to cherish her process.

No cryptic captions. No social media shade. No begging anyone to understand.
She didn't need an audience for her evolution.
She needed a boundary for her energy.

And in that quiet, she built strength.
One unanswered question at a time.
One withheld truth at a time.
One unspoken poem at a time.

Because not every story is meant to be shared while it's still being written —
and **not everyone deserves front-row seats to a woman's rebirth.**

Rule #4: Don't React with Emotions

David was unraveling.
The more Gabrielle stayed silent, the louder he got.
And not just in volume — in tactics.
Angry texts. Drunken voicemails. Long paragraphs laced with guilt and gaslighting.
He was throwing every emotion at the wall, hoping something would stick.

"You left me emotionally, Gabi. You just shut down on me."
"You always wanted the spotlight more than you wanted love."
"You think you're better than me now, huh?"

Gabrielle read the messages with still hands and steady breath.
Didn't flinch. Didn't respond.
She sipped her tea. Lit her candles.
Wrote poetry instead of paragraphs.

Because she had learned:
If someone can control your reactions, they can control your reality.

David was desperate for a reaction —
tears, yelling, rage, *something* to prove he still mattered.
But Gabi wasn't giving him the stage.

She'd spent too long performing emotions just to keep someone else calm.
Now?
She was choosing emotional detachment like armor.

One night he cornered her in the kitchen.
"Answer me!" he snapped. "Why you actin' brand new? I made you!"
Gabrielle turned slow, eyes ice-cold.
"You didn't make me. You just didn't think I'd stop shrinking."

His jaw clenched. "You think ignoring me makes you strong? That's fake power."
She grabbed her notebook and walked past him, voice low but lethal.
"No. Real power is walking through fire without screaming."

And she meant it.
She cried in private.
She bled in metaphors.
She screamed in silence.
But she never gave him the satisfaction of seeing her shatter.

Because real queens don't perform for people who enjoy their pain.
They rise. Quietly. Rebuilt.

And every time she didn't text back, didn't argue, didn't explain — she was reclaiming a piece of her power.

David wasn't in a relationship anymore.
He was shadowboxing a woman who had already emotionally checked out.

Rule #5: Always Be Willing to Walk Away

Always Be Willing to Walk Away is the final, most powerful chapter of Gabrielle's transformation. This isn't **just about physically leaving** — it's about **reclaiming identity, cutting the leash,** and **choosing purpose over pain.**

Gabrielle doesn't walk away broken.
She walks away rebuilt — with poise, clarity, and a spine made of steel.

The night of her comeback performance was electric.
The venue was packed, standing room only.
Women, students, elders — all gathered, hungry for her voice again.
Her name whispered through the crowd like a prophecy.
She hadn't touched a stage in months,
but tonight she was ready —
not to be seen,
but to be heard.

Backstage, she stood alone, wrapped in a soft hoodie and unshakable purpose.
No David.
No texts.

No chaos.
Just peace — and a notebook full of truth.

When she stepped up to the mic, the room fell into stillness.
No music. No introduction.
Just Gabrielle — eyes sharp, voice steady, crown invisible
but undeniable.

And then she delivered the piece that sealed everything.

> *"I found myself beneath your weight —*
> *But Queens don't bloom in shadows.*
> *I cut your leash with a whisper,*
> *And built my kingdom in silence."*

The last word dropped, and the room erupted.
But Gabrielle didn't smile for applause.
She stood tall, let it wash over her —
and then walked offstage like a woman walking out of a burning
house she refused to call home.

That night, she packed.
No drama. No warning.
Just folded the last sweatshirt.
Zipped the final bag.
Took her journal, her mic, and her peace.
And walked out.

David got home to silence.
No note. No fight. No final plea.
Just absence.
And for the first time, he realized:
She hadn't been quiet.
She had been **leaving**.

Because Gabrielle finally understood:
Love should never require you to lose yourself to keep someone else.
And if a man can only love you when you're small,
then he was never your partner —
he was your cage.

She didn't leave out of hate.
She left out of *love* —
for herself,
for her art,
for the women who needed her words,
and for the crown that waited patiently while she remembered her worth.

Closing Reflection: A Crown Unshaken

Gabrielle rose from the wreckage with grace, not rage. Her voice now held more power because it was reclaimed. Her silence had become a sanctuary. Her departure, a declaration. She understood now that sometimes love isn't lost—it's released.

And a Queen's Tru strength?

It's knowing when to put down the mic…

And walk away with the crown.

When You Can't Fully Walk Away: Reality Check
Real talk—
I know some of y'all been reading this like,
"Yeah, I feel all this, I'm ready to bounce,
but what if I **can't** fully walk away?"

What if you got **kids** together?
A **shared life**?
A situation that got **history, bills, custody schedules, and court dates** tied into it?

Yeah… I see you.
This book ain't blind to reality.
This ain't just for the ones who can ghost and disappear overnight.

Sometimes walking away don't mean disappearing.
Sometimes walking away means **reclaiming your power—even if you gotta stay in the same room.**

You might not be able to walk away clean,
but you can still walk away **correct**.
You can shut down the emotional door,
even if the front door gotta stay open for the kids.
Your ex may still be around—**but they don't live in you no more**.

Control the narrative. Protect your peace. Master your role.
Keep it business. Keep it calm. Keep it cool.
Don't argue with messy. Don't chase clarity from anger, but chase clarity from calm.

Don't let your kids grow up watching you beg for respect—they're learning what love looks like from you.

You ain't gotta fight for revenge.
You just gotta **move like a Boss**.
Be unshakable. Be solid. Be **unavailable for drama**.

Because even if you share a child, a past, a place…
you don't have to share your peace.

They might still be part of your story—
But they don't get to **edit your ending**.

You can love your child and not tolerate disrespect.
You can be a great parent and still refuse to be a doormat.
You can share custody without sharing your soul.

So if you can't walk away yet—**stand different**.
Stand taller.
Stand colder.
Stand wiser.

Move with strategy, not emotion.
Speak with control, not chaos.
Give them **no fire to feed off**, and watch how fast they starve.

Because even in the middle of the storm—
You still the one holding the crown.

Love Ain't a Game, Its a Kingdom
Only the Real Ones Make It Past the Gates

In this life, you gon' meet all types. People who come with pretty words, flashy vibes, facade of big energy — but only a few got **real weight** behind what they carry. See, everybody wanna sit at your table, but not everybody bring something worth serving. Some folks come to **feast on your shine**, while others show up to **build the kitchen** with you.

This chapter right here? This for **sorting the real from the fake**, the solid from the shaky, the ones who clap when you win vs. the ones who **helped you get up** after that first fall. Whether it's a **lover you're building with** or a **homie you're riding with**, the Tru Ones don't just show up — they show **consistency, loyalty, and soul-deep presence.**

We not just talking vibes. We talking **tests**, the kind you don't even have to plan — life gon' give them naturally. The way they move in those moments? That's the truth. That's the proof. That's what separates a **temporary character** from a **permanent place in your kingdom**.

So pay attention. Feel the energy. Peep the patterns. And above all — **trust your spirit**. 'Cause real recognize real, and your throne got limited seats.

Part I: 7 Tests to See If They Built for Tru Love — No Crown Without Fire

Aight, real talk. Before you hand someone the keys to your heart — or worse, the keys to your *kingdom* — you better run these tests. Not games. **Tests.** 'Cause love ain't just a vibe or a good night. Love is legacy. Rulership. Divine partnership. And the truth is, not everyone who wants to ride is built for the journey. So here's the 7 real ones to find out if they're down for forever, or just in it for the thrill.

Test #1: Will They Ride or Bail When It Rain?

"Do they only show up when the sun's out, or they stay solid when the storm hits?"

Anybody can smile in the good times. But real ones show up when life get grimy — when money tight, when the future blurry, when your soul feels heavy. If they ain't with you in the dark, they don't deserve your light. A Tru partner rides out the storm — no excuses, no disappearances, just presence.

Test #2: Are They a Mirror or a Mask?

"Do they help you grow, or just pretend to be who you need?"

A real lover reflects your light **and** your shadow. They show you where to heal, not just where to hide. If they always performing, shape-shifting just to keep your attention — that ain't love, that's illusion. You want someone real, not rehearsed. Someone who sees the real you, and shows you the real them.

Test #3: Ten Toes Down or Playing Both Sides?

"When it gets real, are they all in — or switch up when you turn your back?"

You can't build with someone who got one foot out the door. Loyalty means they speak highly of you when you're not around, they protect your name like it's their own, and they don't flinch when things get messy. It's easy to post about you, easy to hold hands in public. But how do they speak about you in private? Do they check people who disrespect you, even if you're not there? Do they protect your image and your energy like it's sacred? Public love is cute. But quiet respect is Royalty. Tru love is steady. No switching teams, no funny business, no snakes in the grass.

Test #4: Can the Silence Hold or Does It Break?

"Is the vibe still real when there's no talk, no performance, just presence?"

Love ain't always loud. Sometimes, it's found in the silence — in how peace feels when y'all just *exist* together. If you can sit in stillness and still feel seen? That's rare. That's gold. That's the kind of bond that don't fade when the noise dies down.

Test #5: Same Path or Split Directions?

"Are y'all building the same future, or walking two different maps?"

A Tru connection is more than chemistry — it's *alignment*. Are your values locked in? Y'all both grinding for purpose, legacy, elevation? If you're building a castle and they chasing chaos, you gon' waste years trying to drag them to your level. Love shouldn't hold you back. It should level you up.

Test #6: Can They Lead Without Ego and Follow Without Shame?

> *"When power shift, do they get petty — or stay graceful in the game?"*

Every real one gon' hit moments where the roles flip — where one of y'all shine more, lead more, earn more. That's life. But ego can kill what love built if they ain't secure in they soul. Can they support you without envy? Can they take guidance without feeling small? A real one ain't threatened by your greatness — they pour into it. Uplift it. Match it. Love ain't a power struggle. It's a throne built for two.

Test #7: Is This Legacy or Just Lust?

> *"Are y'all building something eternal, or just killing time in the moment?"*

Tru lovers think long-term. They're not just in it for the dopamine. They're planting seeds — in business, in healing, in family, in future. Ask yourself: is this love making me **better**, more focused, more fulfilled? Or is it just a beautiful distraction? If it ain't building, it's breaking.

If someone passes these 7? You're not just in love — you're in purpose. You found a partner, not a passenger. Someone you can **build with**, **grow with**, and **win with**.

'Cause at the end of the day, love ain't just about feeling good — **it's about who's still standing with you when the crown gets heavy.**

Part II: 7 Tests to See Who Really Rocking With You — Tru Homie Edition

> *"Everybody claiming 'fam' till it's time to really stand firm. Let's separate the hype from the heavy."*

Test #1: Is Their Loyalty Loud When You Ain't in the Room?

> *"Do they speak your name with respect, or let folks play with it while they stay quiet?"*

A Tru homie don't just dap you up in public — they **defend your name** in private. They not letting no gossip fly, no snake talk that sly sh*t, and they don't rock with folks who throw dirt on your rep. Loyalty is louder **when you not there** to hear it.

Test #2: Can You Bleed Around 'Em and Still Feel Safe?

> *"Can you fall apart in front of 'em and not feel judged or exposed?"*

A real one ain't just there for the wins — they're there for the breakdowns. If you can cry, vent, or go quiet and they don't treat you different, you got gold. **If they weaponize your vulnerability later? That ain't fam — that's a fed.** Cut 'em off and keep moving.

Test #3: Do They Clap for You When It Ain't Their Turn?

"Can they celebrate your shine, even if they still in the dark?"

Some folks cool with you as long as you on their level — but the minute you elevate, they start acting funny. A Tru homie? They cheer you on **even if their season ain't hit yet.** They don't envy your come-up — they **honor it**.

Test #4: Are They Solid or Situational?

"Do they switch sides depending on the setting, or stay the same everywhere?"

A real one's consistent. They don't play roles depending on who's around. Whether it's the streets, the office, the fam cookout or the trenches — **they stand the same**. If you gotta question their energy every time the scene change? That ain't your people.

Test #5: Will They Call You Out Without Tearing You Down?

"Do they correct you in love, or just cosign your mess to keep the peace?"

Tru homies hold you **accountable** — not to control you, but 'cause they believe in your greatness. They'll pull you to the side and say, "That ain't you," with **respect and clarity**. Not shady. Not petty.

Just love disguised as truth. And they would do that by putting the friendship on the line if they have to.

Test #6: Can They Hold Water or Do They Spill Tea?

"Is your business safe with them or are they running their mouth?"

Your Tru ones don't leak your lows for likes. Your secrets don't become stories. They not in group chats with your name in their mouth. **They're the vault.** And if they ever slipped up, it eats at them — 'cause they got **character**, not just vibes. And They would never ever. I mean never, ever, ever, give you up just to get themselves outta messy situations.

Test #7: Are They There When There's Nothing to Gain?

"If you had nothing but a chair and your thoughts, would they still pull up?"

When the lights go off and the party quiet, who's still standing next to you? **No handouts. No favors. No flex.** Just presence. Real friendship don't ask, "What you got?" It asks, "You good?" That's family. That's tribe. Tru vibe!

Real Ones Ain't Many, But They're Everything

Keep your circle tight and your standards tighter. Some folks come with noise. A few come with **loyalty**, **truth**, and **presence**. Don't be afraid to outgrow the fake ones — that ain't disloyal, that's your divine right to protect yourself.

"**Tru homies don't ride for attention. They ride in silence, in truth, in love — all gas, no mask.**"

If They Ain't Real, They Can't Stay
When you know who you are, you stop begging people to stay. You stop breaking yourself into pieces just to keep someone whole. Whether it's your lover or your homie, the ones who are **meant to build with you** — they don't fold when it gets hard.
They **don't switch when it gets real**. They **lock in**, not out.

Your love is sacred. Your loyalty is Royalty.
Don't give it to folks who ain't earned it.

A Tru Lover will **build with you**, not just benefit from you.
A Tru Homie will **protect you**, not just post about you.

Both are rare.
Both are golden.
Both are worth holding — but only if they prove they worth that place.

So keep walking. Keep shining. Keep loving strong but **never blind**.

Only the **Tru Ones** belong.

Final Word: The Throne Is Yours (The Legacy Begins)

You made it, my Kings and Queens. If you've made it this far without skipping any damn pages of this book, without flinching from these raw truths, it means you ain't just skimming through life anymore. You made a choice—to wake the hell up, to rise, to stop being a damn pawn in somebody else's game, a background character in your own saga. And that choice? That's what separates the Royalties from the clowns, the legends from the forgotten, the rulers from the ruled.

A lotta dummies out here still sleepwalking, still begging for crumbs from people who ain't even worth the air they breathing, chasing shadows and validation, living a hollow existence. But not you. You took the hit, you felt the pain, you stared down the darkness in your own soul and in the world, and you turned it into fuel. You got blood on your knuckles and scars on your soul from the battles you've fought and won, but guess what? You still standing, taller and stronger than ever before. That's Real Royalty sh*t. That's the undeniable mark of a Tru sovereign, etched into your very being.

This ain't no fairytale ending. There's no magic wand. No sudden applause, no cheering crowds. Just you and the mirror. Just you and the grind. Just you and the cold, concrete truth. But that's all you ever needed. Because you, my Royal, are the Blessing.

You don't need their validation. You don't need their approval. You don't need permission to walk in your purpose.

The world don't hand out crowns—you gotta build your own, brick by brick, pain by pain, lesson by lesson, sacrifice by damn sacrifice. And when you finally wear it, when you finally claim that inherent power, that divine right to reign, don't lower your head for nobody.

Walk with your chest out, head high, your presence commanding. Speak with your silence, letting your actions echo louder than words. Move like you own the damn block by showing respect and without looking anyone down—because in your story, in your kingdom, you move with purpose. Purpose of growing and achieving that Power and Peace. This is your legacy.

So from here on out, this ain't about proving nothing to nobody. It's about protecting your peace, stacking your purpose, and showing the next generation, showing the world, how a real one moves, how a Tru King, a Tru Queen, builds an unconquerable empire from the inside out.

Respect is earned.

Loyalty is rare.

And love—real love—starts with your damn self.

You ain't just surviving no more. You building. You living. You ruling.

Welcome to your throne. Your reign has begun.

Stay dangerous. Stay grounded. Stay Royal.

Peace!

LETTER TO MY OLD SELF

You didn't know better—you gave way too much,
Loved way too loud, and believed in a touch.
You tried to prove you were worthy of time,
To people who never deserved your shine.

You begged for a love that was already gone,
Not knowing **you** were the blessing all along.

But I forgive you.

I forgive the signs that you chose to ignore,
All the red flags that you let through the door.
For calling it passion when it was just pain,
For dancing in storms and calling it rain.

I forgive you for loving when it was a game,
For waiting on folks who forgot your name.
For lowering your worth just to feel alive,
For shrinking your soul so someone could thrive.

You were trying to live. You were trying to cope.
Building with bricks while you carried no hope.
Trying to patch what was already cracked,
Fixing up others so you'd feel intact.

THE ANTIDOTE

But now?

Now you walk different. You speak with intent.
You spend your peace on what's heaven-sent.
You protect your soul like a loaded vault,
And you know when to dip—it ain't always your fault.

You don't chase. You don't beg. You don't try to explain.
You're done giving energy out in vain.

You've outgrown versions that begged you to stay,
Outlived the lies that stood in your way.
You buried old habits. You shattered the chain.
You looked in the mirror and saw what remained.

You don't just survive anymore—
'Cause you ready to reign.

So this is your reminder—

You ain't too much. They were never enough.
Their love was a lie, and you called the bluff.
Love that drains you? That ain't love at all.
That's a rigged election to make giants feel small.

You don't gotta prove what you already know,
Your worth ain't a maybe. It's bold, and it shows.
Being alone beats being misused,
And peace? That's louder than being pursued.

SUNNY MASTERPEACE

Loyalty's rare—so guard it tight.
If it costs your mind, that price ain't right.
If it breaks your soul or kills your rest,
Then best believe—it ain't your best.

Walking away? That's not defeat.
That's **wisdom** wrapped in steady feet.
The real you don't chase. The real you **chooses**.
The real you don't cry when fake love loses.

If they couldn't see your shine—that's their shame.
You glow regardless. **Keep feeding your flame.**

You ain't broken no more.
You're rebuilt.
Unapologetic.

This is your comeback.
Your Crown.

The Antidote.

Poetic.

Now go remind the world who you are—
Not by shouting…
But by showing your scars…